SYMPOSIA

Eros
&
Thanatos

Books by Melinda Selmys

Sexual Authenticity
An Intimate Reflection on Homosexuality and Catholicism

Sexual Authenticity
More Reflections

Slave of Two Masters

Symposia
Eros & Thanatos

SYMPOSIA

Eros & Thanatos

Melinda Selmys

vulgata

This book is dedicated to Nelly.

FORWARD

This book contains two philosophical dramas which concern the fates and fortunes of the Kirkman clan. The Kirkmans are a modern Canadian family with eight children, mostly grown up. They are not, however, typical Canadians: their parents, Jerome and Mary, have made every reasonable attempt (and many unreasonable attempts) to raise their brood with the values, culture and religion of Ancient Rome.

These dialogues chart a small part of the outcome of this experiment. More importantly they explore the way that Western ideas have developed, the relationship between antiquity and contemporary life, and the continuity of the philosophical tradition since Socrates first bothered his Athenian brethren with his persistent questions about life, love, beauty and God.

◦ EROS ◦

∘ THANATOS ∘

Eros

Dramatis Personae

CATULLUS, *A closeted homosexual.*

GERMANICUS, *His brother, a stoic.*

SHEILA, *Not Germanicus' girlfriend.*

LYDIA, *Elder sister to Catullus and Germanicus.*

JEREMIAH, *Lover to Catullus.*

JUVENAL, *A Darwinian social constructivist, more or less.*

ALI, *A postmodern feminist, allegedly Catullus' girlfriend.*

JEROME, *Jerome Kirkman. Father.*

OPENING GAMBIT

(A fight has broken out at the last chance cafe. Two interlocutors, brothers, sit opposite, staring one another down across a cozy little bistro style table. The first, Germanicus, sits sipping a cup of strong black coffee, back straight, jaw set. Across from him Catullus is leaned back in his chair, toying with an ironic smile as he nurses a crème brûlé latte. They are at war over the nature of the human person and the source of his moral ideals.)

GERMANICUS. The point is, certain acts are contrary to the interior logic of the human person, and as a result they lead to various kinds of personal and moral disorder.

CATULLUS. The "interior logic of the human person" as defined by whom?

GERMANICUS. As defined by nature.

CATULLUS. "Nature" does not speak for herself. Her utterances are as subtle and mysterious as the words of the Sybil...and as subject to multiple interpretations. She has had many interpreters over the years. They have hardly all come to the same conclusions.

GERMANICUS. There's certainly a lot of overlap in their conclusions. I think it's reasonable to suppose that where you find overwhelming agreement between men of good will across cultures you are looking at conclusions which arise from the rational contemplation of nature herself.

CATULLUS. *Sed contra*, Germanicus, human beings are overwhelmingly in the habit of defining the term "men of good will" to mean "people who largely agree with me."

GERMANICUS. I mean that there is widespread agreement between people who are trying to be reasonably objective and approach truth without letting personal considerations interfere.

CATULLUS. *(Shrug)* How can a man entirely absorbed in his own subjective experience possibly approach anything which he could reasonably imagine to be "objectivity." Those who think they have objective truth by the tail are usually oroborous.

GERMANICUS. Is that a word?

CATULLUS. It's a neologism. I mean that the arguments become inevitably circular. Self-referentiality is an inescapable property of all objective truth claims.

GERMANICUS. Is that an objective truth claim?

CATULLUS. Yes. And it's conspicuously self-referencing. As you see.

GERMANICUS. Very amusing. No, seriously, let's say that I put forward a really simple, straight-forward proposition that most people would agree with, like...man is rational by nature. How is that self-referencing?

CATULLUS. That's your idea of a statement that most people would agree with?

GERMANICUS. Most people who understand what the terms mean, yes.

CATULLUS. Well, what do you mean by it?

GERMANICUS. I mean that man is inherently capable of reasoning. That that's the kind of being that he is.

CATULLUS. I see. Well to me this entire "kind of being" notion seems like an an abstract invention. An intellectual *trompe l'oeil.*

GERMANICUS. Catullus, everyone believes in "kinds of beings." You believe that an orange is different from an aardvark. That they're different kinds of things. By nature.

CATULLUS. By convention. They are both basically assemblages of carbon atoms and H_2O with a little of this and a little of that mixed in to give some local colour. The carbon and water and what-not are basically just wavelengths of a primordial energy that we call light. Our minds look upon the light and form the impression of a four legged eater of ants. Then we invent a word to group together similar impressions and thus, presto chango, the category of aardvark is produced.

GERMANICUS. Well in that case a human being is the kind of rational subjectivity that is capable of deducing aardvarks from the primordial light. He's still, by nature, a rational being.

CATULLUS. So the objective truth is that a human person is an absolute subjectivity who uses his reason to produce reality and then imagines that his, or her, productions are objective. Yes, all right. I think I can agree to that.

GERMANICUS. That's not what I said. I wasn't actually agreeing with the wider ontological implications of your thesis. I was just pointing out that even if we were to assume all of your premises we would still get the conclusion that there is objectively such a thing as human nature. I'm saying that it's an inescapable conclusion, not a self-referential fallacy.

CATULLUS. Inescapable for a human being, sure. *Cogito ergo cogito.* I reference myself. There's nothing wrong with that. Circular logic isn't a fallacy, it's the only kind of logic there is. That was my point in the first place.

GERMANICUS. I think you're mistaking the existence of first principles for circularity of argumentation.

CATULLUS. How so?

GERMANICUS. The entire basis of logical reasoning rests on the fact that certain principles are tautologically true. A=A. Existence exists. Reason is rational. Goodness is good.

CATULLUS. But your belief in the relationship between truth and reason is an article of faith. You can't prove it rationally. The system cannot bear within itself the means of its own verification. I think that's Heisenberg. Or maybe Gödel?

GERMANICUS. But your consciousness, and hence your very being, depends on a system of rational thought. It is therefore not only reasonable, but necessary, to believe in reason. Like right now, you're trying to make a rational argument for the irrationality of reason, which you should admit is pretty self-defeating.

CATULLUS. I am not arguing that reason is irrational. I'm arguing that reason and rationality are not necessarily objective measures of truth. Besides, I must obviously exercise reason in order to argue with you, but that's only because you've rigged the deck in your favour and I have graciously agreed to play by your rules. This is not how I would normally approach truth at all.

GERMANICUS. Okay, you want irrational arguments in favour of reason? One: everyone intuitively believes, on a gut level, that reason is the faculty by which men apprehend truth. Two: people who don't believe that truth can be accessed by reason tend to suffer from despair, confusion and existential angst. Three: the practice of rationality produces a sense of interior harmony and equilibrium. Four: reasonable people are more reliable and easier to get along with than unreasonable people. Five: rationality produces order and order is a necessary precondition of beauty. You want more?

CATULLUS. No, because I completely agree that reason feels true subjectively. Just like intuition, and practical goodness, and beauty feel subjectively true. I happen to prefer the aesthetic path myself but I don't deny that reason has a sort of beauty to it. Like a Mondrian: lots of right angles and primary colours. Can't compete with Dali, but it has its charm.

GERMANICUS. Reason is the only way of approaching truth that does not leave man stranded in a sea of conflicting images and impressions. It's the only way of establishing a commonly accepted truth between men of different cultures and traditions. It's not just one way of approaching subjective truth, it's *the* way of transcending subjectivity to arrive at objective truth.

CATULLUS. Provided you believe that the products of your reason conform to some invisible, intangible, unobservable and utterly inaccessible kind of truth which allegedly exists somewhere out there beyond reality as we experience it.

GERMANICUS. No. Not beyond reality as we experience it. In reality as we experience it with our reason. I'm saying that reason is the faculty that puts us in contact with objective truth, in the same way that our optical system is the faculty that puts us in contact with the spectrum of visible light.

CATULLUS. And I can no more prove that there is an objective truth out there, outside of my rational experience of it than I can prove that there is a visible light spectrum out there beyond my experience of sight. Subjectivity is the only demonstrable reality. Everything else requires a leap of faith.

GERMANICUS. And if you make that leap of faith you gain everything. Certainty. Reality. Meaning. Purpose. Sense. Beauty. Other minds. God. If you're wrong you have lost nothing. On the other hand if you believe that your subjective faculties are trapped in an inescapable epistemological hall of mirrors, what do you gain? Nothing. But if you're wrong you lose your opportunity to look upon the face of truth. It's a no brainer.

CATULLUS. But I do stand to lose something, Germanicus. You forget how this argument began. You're trying to argue that I should never again have sex with the man whom I have loved for the last five years. You're arguing that for the sake of an abstract good, which may or may not exist, I should give up a very practical good which brings me pleasure and happiness on a more or less daily basis. It is, as you say, a no brainer.

GERMANICUS. I thought we agreed that we would put aside the practical ends of this discussion and stick to the theoretical aspects...that we would see where the argument led and try to arrive at the truth rather than reasoning backwards from your desire to justify gay sex.

CATULLUS. All reasoning is reasoning backwards. One does what is psychologically necessary to survive, and then one rationalizes it. Reason is just the PR department of the soul.

GERMANICUS. Then why did you agree to the argument in the first place?

CATULLUS. Oh, I don't know. Rationalization seems to be amongst the things that one does for the sake of psychological survival. It's somehow important to think that my reasons can stand up to external scrutiny. I suppose in a sense you're right that the rational system is inescapable.

GERMANICUS. Well if we're going to continue the discussion then you're going to have to provide some sort of basis for making decisions about what is and is not true. This conversation is a waste of time if you have the right to move the goalpost any time I score.

CATULLUS. Fine. We'll discuss it rationally. I'll do you one better than that even: we'll discuss it on the basis of natural law.

GERMANICUS. Uh...Okay...Why?

CATULLUS. Because if I can trounce you on your home turf, playing by your rules, then I'll be able to go away in perfect contentment, certain that your position is full of shit.

[End of Part I]

SICILIAN DEFENCE

(Germanicus' coffee has finally gotten cold – the way he likes it. He cracks his knuckles and downs it in a single protracted gulp. Catullus excuses himself to use the men's room. While he is gone his brother can be seen taking invisible books down from invisible shelves, running his finger along key passages from Aristotle and Aquinas as he brushes up on natural law.)

GERMANICUS. Okay. So according to the natural law there are three basic precepts for practical reasoning. Self-preservation --

CATULLUS. Hold on. I said *I* would give *you* a natural law argument. So sit quiet a moment and listen. Premise one: the human person is, by nature, a spiritual being who is extended into a material existence for the purpose of giving and receiving love.

GERMANICUS. Whose definition is that?

CATULLUS. Mine. And I believe that it is eminently rational. Obviously we have an experience of psychosomatic duality. My intuition tells me that the spiritual or mental aspects of my self are more essentially me than my body: I can conceive of a ghost as my "self," I cannot conceive of a corpse in the same way. I can conceive of the spiritual part of me existing without a body, thinking, reasoning, perceiving forms directly through the imagination, receiving infused knowledge and inspiration from gods and muses. So what is the purpose of the body? To me, it seems clear that it is to allow an escape from the tedious insularity of absolute subjectivism. Bodies permit intersubjective interface between human beings. And why do we seek such interface? Because we do not wish to be lonely. Because we hope to love and be loved.

GERMANICUS. Let me get this straight. You seem to be saying that we're basically disembodied spirits that somehow produce bodies so that they won't be lonely? That seems like a weird assumption.

CATULLUS. Whether we deliberately create them or have them bestowed on us by gods or by demons is totally irrelevant. Everyone past the age of deliberation is perfectly capable of divesting himself of his body at a moment's notice. If he so desires, a straight razor or noose will quickly do the trick. Therefore our bodies are, in an important respect, chosen.

GERMANICUS. But if our bodies are bestowed on us by something or someone else, then they're not ours to do with as we will. If they're just an epiphenomenon of mentality, then we have to get into the question of where our spiritual selves come from. You can't address questions of nature without addressing questions of origin.

CATULLUS. I think that you can make reasonable assertions about what a thing is for without necessarily knowing where it came from.

GERMANICUS. Not with anything sophisticated. Let's say you have a person who has never interacted with any human artifact before. Give the guy a knife, and even if he has no idea of the intention of the knife-maker he'll probably be using it to cut up meat by the end of the day. Give the guy an i-Pod, and he'll probably hang it around his neck as an ornament, or start sacrificing small animals to it. A human person is a tremendously complex entity.

CATULLUS. A tremendously complex *self-aware* entity. And that makes all the difference in the world. I'm not an artifact that I found lying about on the Serengeti. I know what I am for because I know what brings me happiness, fulfilment, pleasure, and joy. I don't need to know who or what lies somewhere over the epistemological rainbow, all I need is the evidence of my lived experience.

GERMANICUS. And you're saying that in your lived experience, the thing that brings you happiness and such is loving and being loved.

CATULLUS. Precisely.

GERMANICUS. Okay, but let's say that you had an experience of loving and of being loved, but it was false. The other person was just taking advantage of you, laughing behind your back, creating an illusion for some ulterior motive. Would you be happy with that?

CATULLUS. Obviously not. I would be unhappy because my natural desire for love was being thwarted.

GERMANICUS. Because the love isn't true. Right?

CATULLUS. Oh, I see. You're trying to smuggle truth into the discussion. I'll concede beauty for you in advance, by the way, just so you don't have to waste time. Truth, obviously, is an important quality of true love. But in so far as truth does not serve love or beauty, I don't give a fig for it.

GERMANICUS. Is that statement true?

CATULLUS. It's honest. Truth and honesty are not exactly the same thing. Truth claims some sort of objective status, whereas honesty, good faith and authenticity are perfectly possible in a purely subjective sense. So I take back what I said about true love. So long as love is authentic, it is worth having.

GERMANICUS. Love and beauty are both impossible without truth. Love without truth just becomes emotionalism, and beauty without truth just becomes sentimentalism. Besides, when you love something, or someone, you love because of something of genuine, enduring value. If the object of love is not truly worthy of love, then loving it will ultimately bring unhappiness and dissatisfaction.

CATULLUS. No. If the object of love is not capable of reciprocating, then it will ultimately bring dissatisfaction. That's why you can't get through life being in love with your stuffed animals. But if the beloved is capable of loving in return, and if they do so, then the love will be satisfying. That's why people are constantly falling in love, marrying, and having happy lives with people who everyone else finds odious. Everyone else is incapable of experiencing the reciprocity of feeling which makes such love valuable.

GERMANICUS. I don't know if that "constantly" happens, but I do know that people very often fall in love, and then fall out of love, and that it makes them miserable. That's why love has to be grounded in something more enduring, more *true*, than mere passion. If it's just subjective feeling it doesn't do what you said it was supposed to do, it doesn't get us out of our insular subjectivity.

CATULLUS. But you're talking about escaping from subjectivity into objectivity. I'm talking about escaping from insularity into relatedness. The former requires truth, the latter merely requires authenticity.

GERMANICUS. I'm talking about the fact that the passions are no basis for a moral system.

CATULLUS. I never said they were.

GERMANICUS. Then what do you mean by love?

CATULLUS. I mean that which allows a person to transcend isolated subjectivity and enjoy communion with another person. Obviously there are numerous different modes of loving, and they are not all reducable to mere emotionalism. Loving another person requires responsibility and perseverance, forgiveness and communication, and all sorts of other things that have nothing to do with the passions.

GERMANICUS. But how are you going to derive an obligation to be responsible, or to persevere, without appealing to objective truth?

CATULLUS. That is how lovers naturally behave if their love is authentic. If love is inauthentic, then there is absolutely nothing at all for anyone to gain through some sort of obligatory perseverance and responsibility. All you get then is an empty simulation of the effects of love, but without love at the heart of it. And there are few things that make people more consistently unhappy than the continuation of the forms of love after love is gone.

GERMANICUS. Then it all comes down to emotionalism. You're hiding behind this language of "authenticity," but what you really mean is that if people feel love then they will do all of these other things that are morally laudable, but if they don't feel love then they won't and they don't have to.

CATULLUS. No. Because love itself is obligatory. It is the only obligation. Once you have set your heart on something you must not be fickle. If you stop "feeling" love, then you have an obligation to delve within yourself and within the relationship until you find it again. That is why lovers take vows, in order to relieve one another of the fear of abandonment. It is also, incidentally, why you are not going to convince me that I ought to give up my love because it is "unnatural." I don't break my promises on the basis of casuistries.

GERMANICUS. You're equivocating between love and sex. I'm not suggesting that you give up love. I'm suggesting that there are cases where the latter is incompatible with the former. But since you're not willing to entertain the notion of objectivity, I'll meet you half-way. I think I can prove, within a framework of intersubjective authenticity, that sometimes sex is a betrayal of love.

[End of Part II]

ZWISCHENZUG

(As the day is growing long, Germanicus and Catullus have relocated to a small pub down the street. Catullus is drinking expensive scotch, neat, because he abhors girly cocktails. Germanicus is drinking vodka, because vodka clears your head and allows you to think straight.)

GERMANICUS. The ends of love always have to be the authentic goods of the beloved. That's why a mother takes her kid in for surgery even if the kid is scared and doesn't want to go. Her love compels her to do what is actually good for him rather than what he wants.

CATULLUS. Isn't that a little paternalistic?

GERMANICUS. I don't see how Mom taking me in to have my jaw fixed was paternalistic. It sucked. But it needed to be done.

CATULLUS. Yes, but you were a child then and she was an adult. She was in a position to see more clearly than you what was necessary. The problem is you're trying to extend that principle to relations between adult human beings, which is the very definition of paternalism.

GERMANICUS. No. I'm just making the point that the authenticity of love is vouchsafed by sincere concern for the good of the other, even in cases where the other might not recognize that good.

CATULLUS. And I am saying that, as an adult, I am in a better position than anyone else to determine what is good for me. I have complete access to all of my experience. I know my circumstances perfectly. I understand what hurts me, what gives me pleasure, and how much. None of those things can be generalized, quantified, or adequately expressed in full to an external authority. My ability to recognize my own good, even if it is not perfect, is better than anyone else's. Hence my right to pursue happiness on my own terms.

GERMANICUS. Okay, but let's say, for example, that Jeremiah was really depressed, and he called you to his bedside and he said, "Catullus, if you love me, go out and buy me a fatal dose of morphine." Would you do it?

CATULLUS. No. But if he called me to his bedside every day for a month, I might.

GERMANICUS. But look at your own argument. You said earlier that the body is the means by which people are enabled to give and receive love. Now you're saying that out of love, you might allow a man to deprive himself of that means – and to do so on the basis of some temporary emotional upheaval that would obviously cloud his judgement. Even if he feels like crap for a whole month, chances are he'll come out of it eventually. So you'd have thrown away years of possible happiness.

CATULLUS. Yes, all right. So I wouldn't. I probably wouldn't have anyway.

GERMANICUS. On the basis that what is really good for him, and what he thinks is good for him, are at odds.

CATULLUS. On the basis that his death would make me savagely unhappy, particularly if I had a hand in bringing it about.

GERMANICUS. That seems a rather selfish argument.

CATULLUS. All human acts are rather selfish. This silly idea that moral goodness consists in the abnegation of the self is just a twisted form of self-serving masochism.

GERMANICUS. Sacrificing yourself for the good of others is self-serving? How are you getting that?

CATULLUS. Sacrificing yourself in order to have the pleasure of knowing that your sacrifice will bring pleasure, joy, or life to those you love is perfectly sane and beautiful. Self-abnegation for the sake of self-abnegation is utterly irrational and perfectly poisonous. I mean...have you ever been a relationship with someone who behaves that way? It's impossible to love them. Their entire world-view is built on the idea that other people are worthy objects of love, ends in themselves, infinitely valuable – but that for some reason they themselves are exempt from the general pattern of human dignity. The only pleasure that such a person is capable of enjoying is the pleasure of thinking of himself as singularly virtuous, usually through some sort of nauseating internal contradiction in which they take pleasure in their own humiliation because they imagine that virtue consists in thinking of oneself as depraved and worthless. Self-serving masochism, as I said.

GERMANICUS. Okay, so you think that Jesus of Nazareth – assuming that his motives and world-view were basically as portrayed in the gospels – was self-serving and masochistic?

CATULLUS. I think that Christ is intensely delighted in human beings. We are his creatures, and like any artist he admires his handiwork and wishes for it to endure, "A thing of beauty, and a joy forever." I also think that's a much more beautiful narrative than the idea that he descended from heaven into a life that he enjoyed not at all in order to grimly sacrifice himself for creatures whose fate is ultimately irrelevant to him. No beloved wishes to to be subject of his lover's disinterest. I think it's a form of violence, really, to claim to love someone on disinterested terms.

GERMANICUS. We are his what?

CATULLUS. Well if you're going to talk about him, you might as well talk about him as if he's real. Vacuous thought experiments are like warts on the face of philosophy.

GERMANICUS. Sorry. For a moment I thought you'd gone over to the dark side. Okay...I see what you're saying. The virtuous man is made happy by the practice of virtue, and that happiness is a significant motivator in terms of doing the good. That's right there in The Republic. I agree. But it's always led me to the conclusion that if I really love someone, I should be concerned not only for my own virtue, which is a precondition of my happiness, but also for their virtue, which is a precondition of theirs.

CATULLUS. How are you defining virtue?

GERMANICUS. As the rational pursuit of the good.

CATULLUS. So if a person was practicing the sort of twisted so-called "virtue" that I was describing before, then you would, out of genuine love, try to persuade him to abandon the practice in favour of pursuing his actual happiness. Yes, I think I could see my way to agreeing with that.

GERMANICUS. Wait just a second. I think I can see where you're going with this, and I think that we need to back up a little. You're going to claim that if your lover, out of a desire to be virtuous, is practicing some sort of chastity, and you think that it's making him unhappy, then you have both the right and the obligation to seduce him. Am I right, or am I jumping the gun?

CATULLUS. If someone has been brain-washed into thinking that their natural desires and inmost longings are immoral, and they've worked themselves into a knot of self-denial, guilt, shame, and self-loathing, heavily spiced with depression, loneliness and sexual frustration, then yes. I mean...seduction is a rather heavy-handed and probably inappropriate way of bringing them out of it. But if you love someone, you can't just sit by and watch them do that to themselves indefinitely.

GERMANICUS. Whoa. And you accused me of being paternalistic?

CATULLUS. I thought you believed that love always pursues the authentic good of the beloved.

GERMANICUS. On what possible basis could you be certain that my sexual ethics are the result of "brain-washing," rather than the result of a free, responsible, adult choice?

CATULLUS. You? Oh. I wasn't talking about you. You seem to get some sort of kick out of being chaste. Like Socrates. I honestly think he derived more pleasure from lying next to Alcibiades, revelling in the fact that he could be so close to the object of his desire without reaching out to pluck its fruit, than he would have felt if they'd just had sex. And Alcibiades got the pleasure of laughing at Socrates about it in public, so all's fair. No. No. There are obviously people for whom chastity really is good, and I wouldn't deny it to them. I just think it's ridiculous of those people to assume that just because they are able to derive joy, happiness, internal equilibrium, and authentic freedom from the practice of abstaining from sex, that therefore everyone else will have the same experience. Especially since everyone else is very emphatic in claiming *not* to have that experience.

GERMANICUS. But Catullus, everyone else hasn't ever really tried it. I mean...I know what it's like when your body is kicking up a temper tantrum, and your passions are all in a stew, and Eros is riding you down like the Big Red Bull, but I really don't think that *you* know what it's like when you get beyond that point, and everything is clear, and you experience what it's like really to be free. Just white-knuckling your way from one desperate masturbatory fall-down to the next, motivated by the fear of eternal punishment, or the feeling that sex will make you dirty, that's not chastity. That's just self-torture. Obviously you wouldn't want to watch someone you loved go through that...but the solution isn't to convince them to just let it all go and sink back into the clutches of lust. The solution is to help them to get through it, to help them reach the point where they're no longer enslaved by sexual desire.

CATULLUS. You mean if you really love someone you should help them get to the point where they no longer wish to express their love for you in the most pleasurable and intimate way possible?

GERMANICUS. I'm saying that if you really love someone, you should want to be able to express your love for them, and to receive their love for you, in freedom. Responsibly. As human beings, rather than as animals. That sex should serve the good rather than being mistaken for the good.

CATULLUS. *(peering past Germanicus towards the door)* Mmm. Well, you'll be glad to know that the object of your chaste indifference is about to join us.

GERMANICUS. *(looking duly alarmed)* What?

CATULLUS. *(stands, waving over a woman with streaky blond hair and too much mascara)* Sheila's here. And I'm sure she'll be fascinated to hear just how much fun you're having being responsibly free of all carnal desire...

[End of Part III]

A MODEL OF DECORUM AND TRANQUILITY

(Sheila hovers awkwardly for a moment at the end of the table, trying to make her skirt miraculously extend down to brush the tops of her knees. Germanicus attempts to make his body conterminous with the wall in order to allow her enough space to sit without risking embarrassing contact between his jeans and her thigh. As she arranges herself, he orders her a drink.)

SHEILA. Hey guys. I saw you through the window. I hope you don't mind me butting in?

CATULLUS. Not at all. I welcome the support. Germanicus has been trying to convince me that it's unnatural for me to have sex with men.

SHEILA. Germanicus! Really? I'm so sorry Catullus. He doesn't mean anything by it. It's just that he has Asperger's syndrome, so when he says things, he can't really relate to the way they make other people feel.

GERMANICUS. Asperger's syndrome? When did I develop that?

CATULLUS. It's all right, Sheila. I have been his brother for quite some time, and I did agree to the argument.

SHEILA. Well he's wrong anyways. Obviously, if you're gay it's natural for you to have gay sex.

GERMANICUS. Don't give me the gay wolf argument. Please don't give me the gay wolf argument. I have far too much respect for you, and if you start talking about lesbian seagulls, my faith in your intelligence is going to be seriously shaken.

SHEILA. It has nothing to do with lesbian seagulls, Germanicus. If someone has a strong, innate desire, going back to the time when they first started to have sexual thoughts, then it's reasonable to think that for them that desire is natural. It just makes sense.

GERMANICUS. So if I have a strong, innate desire to go around bashing people's skulls in with rocks, and it goes back to my early childhood, then that's natural for me?

SHEILA. Sure it is. It may not be right, but it's natural.

GERMANICUS. You're equivocating on the word "natural." I'm talking about "natural" in the sense of "in accord with the ideal-form of a thing."

SHEILA. Oh my god. I remember this argument from when we were studying for my philosophy exam. I just can't get my head around the idea that something can be considered "in accord with nature" when you can't actually find it anywhere *in* nature.

GERMANICUS. It's really not that complicated. The point is that things, whether they're human beings, or moral acts, or tea-kettles, are intended for a specific purpose. I don't care if you believe in god, or in evolution, or if you're a dumb stump football fan who has never entertained a metaphysical speculation in his life, it's just obvious that sex is for procreation.

SHEILA. Obvious how?

GERMANICUS. Look, I know this may be a really abstruse and difficult point, but the reproductive system is a system, right?, which is meant for reproduction.

SHEILA. If you're a frog.

GERMANICUS. What?

SHEILA. Not if you're human being. Look, it's like saying that the mouth is part of the digestive system and that therefore it is unnatural to use it for any purpose except eating. That talking, and smiling, and kissing are contrary to the "natural law." It's absurd. Human bodies aren't dishwashers. They don't come with a sticker that says "Warranty void unless used in accord with the manufacturer's instructions."

GERMANICUS. No. But you can clearly see that certain things are bad for you. That they're a misuse of the body. Like smoking, for example, is a misuse of the lungs.

SHEILA. Right. Which is a really strong argument against the idea that sex is only for procreation.

GERMANICUS. How do you figure?

SHEILA. Because Germanicus, most people aren't like you. I mean, I remember the first time that we had this argument, you totally convinced me you were right. Everything you said made so much rational sense. But when I tried to do it in practice, it was just a mess. I felt lonely, I felt depressed, I felt like I was missing out on life. Eventually I got so up-tight that I couldn't even function, I was just spending all of my time and effort doing nothing except trying *not* to have sex. People can't live like that. And talking to people other than you, I know there isn't something wrong with me. Almost no one can go that long without doing something, even if it's just masturbation. But on the other hand, there's no way that I could just start procreating all the time. I mean, back before they had contraception, when people believed that it was a sin to have sex without trying to have a baby, one of the leading causes of death amongst women was childbirth. My body is not intended to be pregnant all the time. It's not designed to have a baby every time that I have sex. I mean, if nature is so determined that all sex must be procreative, then why am I only fertile three days in a month? Why do pregnant women still want to make love? Why is the way that it actually works in reality so utterly divorced from the way that it is in Plato's head?

GERMANICUS. I didn't say that there's not more to it than just reproduction. I mean...obviously the multitudes account it blissful, and there's all the gooshy emotional stuff, and I understand that if someone gets married that probably they're going to need to have sex with their spouse more often than is strictly necessary to have children, because otherwise their spouse is probably going to start looking for someone else. But --

SHEILA. Germanicus...honey...listen. I know that this doesn't really make a lot of sense to you, but that's not how other people see it. Most people don't have sex with their wives just to prevent adultery. Most people have sex with their wives because they really want to, because it makes them happy. It's not a chore. Now I know that I used to accuse you of being erotophobic, and I've realized that that's unfair and actually kind of judgemental. There's a woman in my gender-studies class who identifies as asexual, and she made me realize that for some people not having sex really is natural. And that's okay. But you need to understand that for most people that's not how it is. And that's okay too.

GERMANICUS. I'm not erotophobic, or asexual, and I hate when you diagnose me with disorders. Look, I understand that this is something that people really like to do. I'm sure that whenever I get married, I'll be really happy to do it too. In fact, I have absolutely no doubts on that account. However, I think that until I am ready to be in a relationship that is specifically intended for the purpose of having children it's totally irresponsible for me to do something that could get a girl pregnant with a baby that I'm not ready to look after.

CATULLUS. *(laughing)* And how likely do you think it is that I'm going to get my partner pregnant? Or visa versa, as the case may be.

SHEILA. Catullus is right, Germanicus. And it doesn't just apply to people who are gay. I mean...if you're not ready to have kids, and you're really not asexual, what would be wrong with mutual masturbation? Or oral sex?

CATULLUS. Or, for that matter, the "unnatural act"?

GERMANICUS. *(texting for back-up under the table)* What would be wrong with it, is that it's not what sex is for. I mean, if I were married, then even sex that didn't actually lead directly to procreation would still be ordered towards the good of my family...it would keep my wife happy, and my marriage intact, and, yeah, okay, admitted, it would also probably help to keep me frosty and kindly endeared towards my wife, which would certainly be in the interests of my kids.

CATULLUS. Ah, but let's imagine that the woman who will one day be your wife is, purely hypothetically, waxing melancholic one night. For years she's been throwing herself at you, and for years has found herself rebuffed, and now she has come to the end of the line. "He will never love me!" she cries, and cursing Plato in her heart she goes out on the town. It could happen, couldn't it Sheila?

SHEILA. It's a distinct possibility.

CATULLUS. There can be no doubt. A girl can only take so much rejection. So now, overcome with loneliness and sexual frustration, she becomes easy prey for unscrupulous mongrels of every stripe. She is plunged into a cesspool of sin, syphilis, sodomy and snake porn. Would that be in the interests of your future family?

GERMANICUS. Don't be absurd. Of course it wouldn't. But that's why it's so important for people to practice self-control.

CATULLUS. Yes. But knowing, as you do, that Sheila is not going to suddenly become a Platonist overnight, wouldn't the responsible thing to do, the loving thing to do, the thing to do in the best interests of your possible future children, wouldn't the best thing be for you to be the one to take her home?

GERMANICUS. I thought we were talking about the morality of homosexual sex. Not about whether Sheila and I should...

CATULLUS. Make the two-backed beast?

GERMANICUS. Catullus, I'm going to kill you.

SHEILA. Exactly why is it okay for you to have a philosophical argument about your brother's sexuality, but not about your own?

GERMANICUS. *(Cell phone beeps. Germanicus checks his messages and sighs with relief.)* Praise Athena. The cavalry is on the way.

CATULLUS. Cavalry?

GERMANICUS. Lydia, apparently, has all her kids in bed so she can join us for a drink. And you won't be able to beat her with cheap psychological tricks.

CATULLUS. *(Suddenly becoming very pale and agitated)* You asked Lydia to join us? Germanicus! Oh gods, I knew I never should have come out, not even just to you. That if I ever told anyone, you'd all know within a week. But I did think at least it would be done behind my back, and you'd all feel compelled to pretend you didn't know.

GERMANICUS. Sorry. Heat of battle. I didn't think about it...But I haven't told her anything. Just that an argument's afoot.

CATULLUS. All right, Sheila, here's the deal. I have never so much as contemplated having sex with men. We are having a completely abstract discussion. I have a girlfriend, and I'm certainly not gay.

[End of Part IV]

QUARTET

(Catullus leans to the side, trying to see through the window. It's one of those winter nights where the frost clings to the edges of the glass, and the world is refracted into a crystalline structure of indistinct and shifting colours. Sheila kicks Germanicus under the table and leans supportively towards Catullus.)

SHEILA. Catullus...I don't understand why you feel ashamed of your sexuality.

CATULLUS. I don't. I just don't want Mom to know.

SHEILA. But don't you think she needs to accept you as you really are?

CATULLUS. Mom does not accept people as they really are. *(He raises his hand and waves)* Isn't that right Lydie?

(Lydia joins them dressed in a beige wool coat and a vaguely medieval dress)

LYDIA. Isn't what right?

GERMANICUS. That Mom doesn't accept people as they are.

LYDIA. I know. She totally doesn't. She wouldn't talk to me for years after I got baptized.

SHEILA. That's really weird. Why not?

GERMANICUS. Christianity's a slave religion. It brought down the Empire. It set back civilization for two-thousand years.

LYDIA. You don't still believe that?

GERMANICUS. No, not really. JC's philosophy has some interesting points.

LYDIA. Yeah. Okay. We'll take that up another time. So I heard there was a debate. What's the resolution?

CATULLUS. Be it resolved that certain sexual acts are, by nature, to be morally proscribed.

LYDIA. Okay. So I'm pro, and so is Germanicus. Sheila...I'm going to guess is not. Catullus...I don't know what Catullus thinks. I don't think I've ever heard you mention sex.

CATULLUS. I'm playing devil's advocate, backing Sheila up.

LYDIA. Okay. Sounds fun. Let's go.

GERMANICUS. Well, I suppose we'd better start by bringing you up to speed. *(Lydia is treated to a brief play by play, with all of the personal aspects of the argument excised.)*

LYDIA. So Catullus' argument, tell me if I get this straight, is that if you know someone you love is going to commit a sexual sin if you don't have sex with them, then you should have sex with them so that they don't get HIV?

CATULLUS. Assuming, of course, that you would want to do so.

LYDIA. Right. So what if this person that you love already has HIV? And what if after you have sex, they decide that they don't love you back? Then you're screwed.

CATULLUS. What if you love them enough that you're willing to assume that risk?

LYDIA. Then ask them to marry you.

SHEILA. What if they're not willing to get married?

LYDIA. Then why should you be willing to have sex? So that they can leave you with an unplanned pregnancy and an STD? No. I don't think so.

SHEILA. So you think it's realistic that people are not going to have sex until they're ready to get married? Are you going to go back to marrying kids off when they're thirteen?

LYDIA. No. But I thought we were talking about what people should do, not what they do do.

SHEILA. So what do you think somebody should do if they're not planning to get married for a while, and it's not realistic that they're not going to have sex.

LYDIA. Make it realistic.

SHEILA. How?

LYDIA. Practice.

CATULLUS. Practice what? How on earth are you supposed to "practice" not doing something?

LYDIA. By, you don't do it for as long as you can, and after you fall down, you go back to not doing it for as long as you can, until you get good at it.

CATULLUS. But suppose that you're at the end of the line. Suppose you've already done this "for as long as you can" schtick, and now you're deciding how best to fall down?

LYDIA. In my experience, when you get to "how best to fall down" there's no deciding involved. If you're still making rational decisions, you can keep going.

SHEILA. So your theory is that people should never make reasonable decisions about their sexuality?

LYDIA. That's not what I said. I was just saying that Catullus' psychology makes no sense. It assumes that you're not really trying. That you're intending to fail. Which...if you intend to fail, you will.

GERMANICUS. How about, if you really can't go any longer, masturbate. I know it's gross, and unnatural, but at least it's safe.

CATULLUS. Lydia's a Catholic, Germanicus. They think that's a mortal sin.

LYDIA. Yes. But even with mortal sins, some are worse than others. And if you really can't help it, then it's not a mortal sin.

CATULLUS. Mmm hmmm. But the sin of fornication is less grievous than the sin of masturbation, at least according to Aquinas. So Germanicus is wrong.

LYDIA. Where are you getting that?

CATULLUS. I looked it up once. I needed to prove that your church's sexual ethics don't make sense. There was a lot riding on it at the time.

LYDIA. You mean you Googled it. 'Cause if you read the Summa, you'd know that what you're saying is totally an oversimplification.

CATULLUS. All right, Lydia. You want something where I actually read the primary source documents, how about the teaching on natural family planning?

LYDIA. What about it?

CATULLUS. It's balls, that's what. Complete balls! Irrational, self-contradicting, utterly arbitrary, and perfectly insane. In a word, balls.

SHEILA. Besides which, it doesn't work.

LYDIA. Okay. Hold back. One at a time. Catullus first.

CATULLUS. All right. The theory here is that somehow sex is procreative even when it cannot possibly procreate, and that couples can be "open to life" even when they're determined not to let life in.

LYDIA. Point one: wrong. The theory is that the acts are of a procreative type.

CATULLUS. Language games, Lydia. It's nothing but a language game. And a language game of the worst, most sophistical kind. Only a scholastic suffering from severe academentia could possibly believe that a naturally sterile act is "of the procreative type."

LYDIA. But I'm not talking about *naturally* sterile acts.

CATULLUS. Lydia, the female body is fertile and barren on a cyclical basis. It is how you are designed by nature, not by artifice or by convention.

LYDIA. Duh, obviously. That's why natural family planning is *natural.*

CATULLUS. And it is also why sexual acts committed during the infertile period are *naturally* sterile. Every bit as sterile, *by nature*, as the "unnatural act."

LYDIA. Catullus, unnatural acts are never procreative. They are by nature closed to life. They cannot produce children. Normal sex can produce children. That's the difference.

CATULLUS. "Normal" sex during pregnancy cannot produce children any more than a cat can give birth to a mouse.

LYDIA. But that's just because of circumstance.

CATULLUS. It is because of the nature of the female body and of her womb.

LYDIA. Yes, but the act --

CATULLUS. Concerns the body. The entire body. In a fairly intimate way.

LYDIA. -- is not being intentionally closed to life by either the woman or the man.

CATULLUS. If two men have sex, neither of them intentionally closes the act to life.

LYDIA. But the act is by nature closed to life.

CATULLUS. So which is it? The act must be procreative by nature, or by intention? Where is this goalpost? It moves each time I shoot.

LYDIA. Germanicus, where's the rest of my team here? Hello? Can't you help out?

GERMANICUS. Sorry, Lydia. He's right. Sex during pregnancy is unnatural. And so is NFP.

[End of Part V]

STALEMATE

(Captain Subtext Transmitting: Catullus is tentatively putting his foot out of the closet with Germanicus so he can see how his family will react to his homosexuality. Germanicus is trying to maintain his rationalistic convictions in the face of the temptation posed to him by Sheila. Sheila is hoping that Germanicus will stop maintaining his rationalistic convictions and ask her out. Lydia is utterly oblivious and thinks it's just a rational debate.)

SHEILA. You think sex during pregnancy is unnatural? Seriously?

CATULLUS. Germanicus, nobody has believed that in 1600 years.

GERMANICUS. Truth doesn't change. It is eternal. It is immutable. It is fixed. 1600 years do not have any bearing on it whatsoever.

SHEILA. But just because they believed something in ancient Rome that doesn't mean it's the eternal truth.

GERMANICUS. It has nothing to do with Rome. It's a rational argument: you don't sow seed in a barren field. It just doesn't make sense.

SHEILA. I am a person, not a field.

GERMANICUS. It's an analogy. It means you don't do things when they won't conduce towards their ends.

SHEILA. But why is pleasure not an end of sex? Or love? Or even just plain fun?

GERMANICUS. For the same reason that you don't open beer bottles with your wedding ring. The thing that sex is actually for is too important to misuse it just for fun.

SHEILA. So love isn't important?

GERMANICUS. Love is not sex!

SHEILA. But sex expresses love.

GERMANICUS. No. The responsible use of sex expresses love. Being willing to bear another person's children expresses love. Being chaste so that you don't make your spouse sick expresses love. Practicing self-control so that you will actually be in rational possession of your faculties and able to make decisions for the good of another person expresses love. Sex without responsibility just expresses passion, which is often antithetical to love.

SHEILA. But how is sex during pregnancy irresponsible? Or sex between two men who are committed to one another?

LYDIA. Time out. You're all missing the point. The natural law is not supposed to be a series of hair-splitting casuistries. It's supposed to be a consolidation of the wisdom of the ages on the question of how to live a happy life. It's like a recipe for happiness that has been perfected by generations of your foremothers.

CATULLUS. Cute. But what if "the wisdom of the ages" makes me unhappy? What if it's a recipe for brownies and I'm allergic to chocolate?

LYDIA. I realize that that looks like a really strong argument. It is a really strong argument. But give me a moment and I'll try to explain. Okay. It is often the case that people think they will be made happy by things that really make them unhappy. Like you remember that guy I dated, Mark?

GERMANICUS. We all remember Mark.

LYDIA. Right. And I thought that he was just the cherry on the cake, but everyone else could see that he was a Total Loser. By the time I figured that out, we'd already had sex, and now I still have images of him come up in my mind when I'm trying to make love to Tom. Gross. Because I thought I knew what would make me happy and I didn't have a clue. I totally should have listened to Dad.

SHEILA. But Lydia, everyone can see that gay people are happier if they have a partner, and less happy if they don't. I mean, whether or not a person has someone to love is a really standard index of the likelihood of suicide, it's a really common predictor of happiness or unhappiness.

LYDIA. I know. But have you seen old gay guys? I know, I shouldn't say this, it's horrible, but it's true. It's really sad. Because they put all of their chips down on that one horse, and most of the time it doesn't place. I used to volunteer at a hospice where there were guys there dying of AIDS with no one to visit them. The gay community had used them up, spit them out, and it was terrible.

CATULLUS. I've met "old gay guys," and that isn't my experience.

LYDIA. Whoa. You took that awfully personally.

CATULLUS. I'm not taking it personally, it was an offensive thing to say! And in any case, there are plenty of straight people in exactly the same boat. Go to any old folk's home on the planet and you'll find them there in droves.

LYDIA. Yeah. The ones who contracepted all their kids away. I mean, Catullus, have you ever, in your entire life, met an old woman with a horde of great-grandchildren who really regrets having chosen that life? Never! Doesn't happen. Having kids is like investing in your future happiness and the happiness of generations to come.

SHEILA. But gay people don't have that option.

GERMANICUS. Sure they do. Look, I know that this is politically incorrect but it happens to be a fact: most of the gay people throughout most of history were heterosexually married. And most of them managed to pay the marriage debt. This whole meme that says gay men can't have straight sex is almost entirely untrue. It's a politically convenient argument to try to make a moral hard-case out of people's carnal desires.

SHEILA. So you think that people should marry people that they're not attracted to and don't love, just so that they can have children?

GERMANICUS. Love is an act of the will. It's not a feeling. I mean, look at all of the other family relationships we have. I don't love Catullus because I saw him one day across the play room and my heart leapt in my chest and winged babies started playing heavenly music over our heads. I love him because he's my brother and I have a fraternal obligation to do so. Obviously I feel affection as well, but the feelings are a result of the act of will, not *visa versa*. This whole social experiment where marriage is based on feelings has been a spectacular disaster because it roots love in something purely temporary and involuntary.

SHEILA. Okay, so when you finally decide that you're ready to get married, you're going to go to your father and get him to find you a suitable woman, a virgin with a dowry who wants to have a dozen kids, and you'll settle down and make it work whether you like her or not?

GERMANICUS. Well...no. But it would probably be better if I did.

LYDIA. Germanicus, that's just nonsense. You shouldn't marry someone you don't love. And gay guys shouldn't marry women just so they can have kids. That's just a disaster waiting to happen.

CATULLUS. So what, in your opinion, ought they to do?

LYDIA. Lots of people live happy lives without getting married. They should form friendships that are stable and responsible, and not based on lust.

CATULLUS. Why is what you feel for Tom "love" and what...a gay man feels for another gay man is "lust"?

LYDIA. If it's not lust, why is the gay community obsessed with sex? I mean, they do they parade around half-naked every year. And it is a notoriously promiscuous sub-culture. Doesn't that suggest that something is not right? If these relationships were as fulfilling as they're supposed to be, wouldn't they be overwhelmingly lasting and monogamous?

CATULLUS. Oh, you mean like marriage? What is the divorce rate again? About fifty percent? And the rate of adultery is similar I hear.

LYDIA. In a self-indulgent, contraceptive culture, yeah. But if you look at the marriages of people who follow the natural law, they're like...I don't remember the statistic, but it's well over ninety percent stable.

SHEILA. Because people who follow the "natural law" are almost 100% Christians who don't believe in divorce, so if they're unhappy in their marriages they stick it out for god.

GERMANICUS. If people are unhappy in their marriages they should figure out how to be responsible for their own happiness, not break their most solemn promises to go scrounging after greener grass on the other side.

SHEILA. How can you be happy with someone who you don't love anymore?

LYDIA. How can you be happy when you can't depend on the most important relationship in your life?

CATULLUS. How can you be happy if you can't have that "most important relationship" at all?

GERMANICUS. Why can't you have that relationship, and just not have sex?

SHEILA. Why would you deny one of life's greatest pleasures to yourself and to the person that you love?

LYDIA. For the sake of something higher.

CATULLUS. Higher than love?

GERMANICUS. Higher than sex.

SHEILA. You mean like god?

LYDIA. Yes. I do mean God.

CATULLUS. But why should God object?

GERMANICUS. For the sake of truth.

(This is where the waitress comes over to recharge the glasses.)

GERMANICUS. Look. It's a well established fact, known throughout all cultures and all times except our own, that sexual desire has the ability to seduce men away from the Good, the Beautiful and the True. For the sake of sex, men betray their loved ones. For the sake of sex they endure ugliness and depravity. For the sake of sex they deny their gods and abandon reason. You therefore must have some way of conforming sexuality to the demands of right reason. You do that by asking "What is this for? What is it's proper use? How can I make sure that I am acting as a free and rational agent, not just going on blind instinct towards whatever feels good?" And I think it's obvious that the purpose of sex is the procreation of the species. That is a genuine good, and if you pursue it rationally, without subserving yourself to pleasure, you avoid the pitfalls that I outlined above...

SHEILA. But pleasure *is* good. People are pleasure-seeking by nature, that's just how we are. Even your rationality, your morality...why do you value these things? Because you enjoy the pleasure of "interior equilibrium." Because you enjoy the pleasure of feeling like you're a rational and virtuous person. Because, and I'm sorry to say this Germanicus, you enjoy the pleasure of feeling like you're better than other people. And if those are the things that really make you happy, that's okay for you. But other people want to be held, want to be loved, want to be made love to. That's what we genuinely want and it's what we freely pursue. That's not irrational, or ugly, or depraved...

LYDIA. No, of course it's not. But pleasure is not the highest good. It's a finger that points us towards the highest good. The things that bring us pleasure do so because they're an image of God. Sex isn't just a rubbing together of body parts or a burst of chemical excitement in the brain. It's not even just a way of feeling close to another person. It's a way of being in communion so intense and so incredible that it's able to make new life. It's literally an image of the Holy Trinity. Is the desire for that bad? Of course not. It's really, really good. But you have to understand it in its proper context as something that actually leads us towards the Good, the Beautiful and True...

CATULLUS. Well at least your not hiding behind some specious argument, pretending that it's "rational" and "natural" and nothing to do with religion. I mean, religious proscription I can understand. Don't eat pork. Don't drink liquor. Shave your head. Never cut your hair. Wear a funny hat. Cut off a piece of your dick. Every religion has to have difficult precepts as a way of gauging whether or not one's adherence is sincere. Arbitrary formal impositions that give shape to moral life − I believe in that. I fast when I'm calling on the Muse, I don't produce kitsch no matter how much money I owe, and I will not abandon my vows even if it leads me to death...

* * *

GERMANICUS. You believe in arbitrary laws, but not objective ones?

* * *

SHEILA. You care more about your virtue than the people that you love?

* * *

LYDIA. You would trade ephemeral pleasure for the good of your eternal soul?

* * *

CATULLUS. Why would God tell me one thing in my heart and another in your law?

(Although the conversation continues on into the wee hours of the morning, no further progress is made.)

[End of Part VI]

BLACK AND WHITE

(*Morning light spills through a salvaged stained-glass window onto a slightly worn parquet floor. Catullus is curled up in a chair, sketch-book in hand, trying to capture the particular way that the sunlight is cupped by the silvery curls of an old man's beard. The man, Jeremiah, picks reluctantly at a bowl of blueberries.*)

CATULLUS. Jeremiah...

JEREMIAH. Yes, Catullus.

CATULLUS. Do you honestly believe that what we do is wrong?

JEREMIAH. I assume you mean the sex? Yes, I think it's wrong...

CATULLUS. Why?

JEREMIAH. We've discussed this before. It never goes anywhere, so unless something has changed I don't see what you're hoping to gain.

CATULLUS. It's just something Germanicus said. He accused me of seducing you. Not in those words, of course, Germanicus is one of those charmingly inept people who never really understand what they're saying. That's why it bothers me, because it's not really his sort of thought – which means that probably some god or other put it in his mouth.

JEREMIAH. I see. I've always assumed that when you seduce me you're aware that that's what you're doing.

CATULLUS. Of course I'm aware of it...but...he said it like it's not a game. Like I'm violating your conscience and undermining your free will or something.

JEREMIAH. And you want me to mollify your conscience by explaining why I think homosexual sex is wrong so that you can shoot my arguments full of holes and feel justified in continuing as you were.

CATULLUS. No. I actually intend to listen this time. I'm going to try to seriously understand your point of view. Promise.

JEREMIAH. Well it's a sin.

CATULLUS. Simple as that?

JEREMIAH. Simple as that. Either you can accept it on my authority, or you can wait and find out for yourself.

CATULLUS. That's completely unfair and no kind of argument. You're older, so you're right. Well I can find old people who agree with me too you know.

JEREMIAH. Catullus, I can give you proper arguments if you want them. Maybe they'll work for you, but I doubt it.

CATULLUS. Why's that?

JEREMIAH. Because they didn't work for me, and I was a lot more committed to making them work... I spent eighteen and a half years trying to make them work, and I've got nothing to show for it except an annulment and a son who won't even use my last name. That's why I don't think they'll help. I can still run through them if you like.

CATULLUS. Can you give me a list of titles to see if any of them interest me?

JEREMIAH. There's the complementarity argument. The argument from aesthetics. The argument from St. Paul. The argument from the Church fathers. The argument from the obligation to perpetuate the species. The argument from the irrationality of lust. The argument from slavery to the passions. The argument from the interior logic of sexuality. The argument from the good of the society --

CATULLUS. I've heard all those. They're the arguments that I shot down last time.

JEREMIAH. I've got one I made up myself based on McLuhan's theory of media. It has to do with the person becoming a servomechanism of his sexuality. The idea is that when sex as a medium reverses its donative and procreative potentials, it becomes rapacious and destructive. Instead of the person being an end in himself and sex being a medium for the creation of ends in themselves, sex becomes an end in itself and consequently a medium for the destruction of the person... I think I kept my marriage going a full extra year with that one.

CATULLUS. *(Golf clap)* Very clever, Miah. You're right, it doesn't help.

JEREMIAH. The reason the arguments don't help is that they're mostly arguments in favour of the beauty and goodness of heterosexual marriage. But if you're married to a woman who won't sleep with you because she thinks you're a disgusting pervert, and if it's hard to argue with her because the truth is you can't sleep with her without imagining that she's a boy, then there's really no theological abstraction that's got a chance.

CATULLUS. Yes, I can see that without having to put myself and some poor woman through 18 years of hell. But given that that is your experience, why on earth do you think that homosexuality is wrong? You have to have a reason. It can't be just...because.

JEREMIAH. Catullus, it's a sin, and it's punishable by death. God knows why. I don't claim to know.

CATULLUS. AIDS is not a punishment for homosexuality. If God is trying to say anything with it – which I think is a dubious proposition – it's that people shouldn't be recklessly promiscuous.

JEREMIAH. Well it's certainly a sin for me to place your life at risk.

CATULLUS. "As though to breathe were life."

JEREMIAH. "Life piled on life is all too little and as one to me." Yes, I know. But your life is not just your own.

CATULLUS. Yes, I realize. "It belongs to God."

JEREMIAH. I mean it also belongs to your father, and to your siblings, and to posterity. If you die young because of me, I have no doubt that I will be held accountable for all of the works of art that you could have produced if I'd kept my pants on.

CATULLUS. Jeremiah, if you had kept your pants, I would have been left to learn art from Ms. Macintire. Assuming I'd survived the ordeal, I'd probably be staging non-object non-event works for the Ontario Arts Council or producing animated goddesses to sell tampons.

JEREMIAH. I would have taken you on as my apprentice even if you hadn't seduced me you know.

CATULLUS. No you wouldn't have. You were terrified. I was an occasion of sin. An occasion, in fact, of the precise sin that destroyed your marriage. A beautiful boy, a student, a constant source of temptation, and if you got caught, probably a lawsuit and jail time. I wasn't worth it.

JEREMIAH. You were worth it. That's why you're still here.

CATULLUS. I know I was, but you did need convincing. You were worth it too, so let's drop all of this nonsense about how much harm you've done me and how you're going to have to account to the Creator for it. Without you I was a lonely teenager with loads of talent, no skill, and a morbid fascination with the possibility of self-slaughter. Without me you were a miserable old sodomite who had lost his faith in God, humanity, and beauty, who produced commercial bullshit in order to pay for the pleasures that kept him numb. I would add that you got that way by trying to do what your church told you to.

JEREMIAH. Not exactly. You have to understand, Catullus, I didn't end up there by being a good Catholic. I became that way by trying to be a good legalist. There's a difference. You can't please God simply by following rules anymore than you can make a masterpiece by doing a paint-by-number.

CATULLUS. That's my argument! You can't steal it!

JEREMIAH. Really? I thought I heard it in a sermon.

CATULLUS. No. You heard it from me the last time we had this fight.

JEREMIAH. Well, then it was a more productive fight than I thought. I've since considered what you said about legalism, and it makes sense out of a great many things that I found it impossible to forgive God for.

CATULLUS. I didn't think men were supposed to 'forgive' God. I thought we were supposed to grovel in humble supplication, beat our breasts and cry "*Mea culpa, mea culpa, mea maxima culpa!*"

JEREMIAH. Mmm. But it's impossible to really recognize your own fault in something until you've forgiven the other party. For example, until recently I found it impossible to forgive the Church for giving Dorothea her annulment. I felt like they'd put the rubber stamp on her unforgiveness and declared all of my best efforts to be null. I still went through the charade of feeling guilty, but really I felt like I'd done everything possible and God was being unfair. That made it impossible to repent.

CATULLUS. But Jeremiah, the church *is* being unfair. You did do everything possible, and the reason that you failed was that the standard was utterly unreasonable.

JEREMIAH. You can never achieve anything great unless you're striving towards an impossible standard.

CATULLUS. I have no problem with that, provided it's understood that the impossible standard is an ideal. The problem with Catholic sexual morality is that you have to be a Saint just to get a passing grade.

JEREMIAH. No. You just have to be ready to admit that you're not a Saint.

CATULLUS. Yes, but what's the point in it? You strive towards the standard, you discover it's impossible, and then you despair. Where do you go from there?

JEREMIAH. You only despair if you're more concerned with following the rules than with trying to have a relationship with God. I've had students like that...only interested in their grades, not in the work. You can't learn anything that way.

CATULLUS. No...I see that. I suppose it's really that the standard isn't just unreasonable, it's insane. It's not even possible to imagine your marriage as anything other than a travesty. It was clearly ill-conceived from the beginning.

JEREMIAH. Yes...that's true. Probably that's why they annulled it. I'd never thought of it that way.

CATULLUS. So even your church acknowledges that your marriage was a sham, but you still think that homosexuality is a sin. Where does that leave us? What is this golden ideal that we're supposed to be chasing in order to achieve great things?

[End of Part VII]

THE BLACK KNIGHT

(A phone rings in an a motel room halfway across the province where Juvenal, Catullus' older brother, is in the shower. Lydia is calling. Shocked and slightly embarrassed at the thought of talking to his big sister without even a towel, Juvenal throws on a bathrobe and answers his phone. Opening pleasantries are exchanged, and then Lydia gets down to the point of her call.)

LYDIA. Okay, so this is going to sound crazy...but I think that Catullus might be gay.

JUVENAL. Astounding Holmes! What incredible sequence of deductions brought you to that conclusion?

LYDIA. So you think so too? Do you have proof?

JUVENAL. We've reached the point where even you have noticed. Q. E. D.

LYDIA. That's not fair. I mean real proof.

JUVENAL. How about you start by telling me what put you on to him?

LYDIA. Okay. So we're in a bar, having a conversation with Germanicus and Sheila about the morality of sex. Catullus claims that he's just playing devil's advocate, but he seems pretty invested...

(Juvenal sits, picks up the complimentary pen and paper and takes a note in an indecipherable script.)

*   *   *

(Meanwhile, Catullus has been forced to cut his conversation with Jeremiah short because his date has arrived to pick him up for Saturnalia. He disappears upstairs and returns wearing a long black coat which covers up his formal wear: the traditional toga virilis which his mother made for his sixteenth birthday. He and Ali talk in the car as they drive to Castle Kirkman.)

ALI. So, I was talking to Sheila and she said that she thought that you might be coming out...

CATULLUS. *Sheila?* I didn't think that you and she had a relationship outside of my parents' house.

ALI. She thought it was important to get in touch with me. She was worried that I might not know about you...that you might be stringing me along. She's actually afraid that her boyfriend is two-timing her and she's projecting that onto us.

CATULLUS. Ah. Well that explains why she's throwing herself at Lord Stoic again. I'm half tempted to take her aside and give her lessons in how to carry out a proper seduction. She could have him by the end of the week if she went about it the right way. And it would be *so* satisfying to see his vaunted "self-possession" cut down.

ALI. I think it's probably a lot more fun to imagine that than it will actually be when it happens.

(Time passes.)

ALI. Do you mind my asking why you decided to come out to him?

CATULLUS. Temporary madness. I saw a woman at the mall selling Christmas cards and bric-a-brac for PFLAG in support of her gay son. I had a Hallmark moment and came down with a severe case of coming-out-itis.

ALI. That might have happened, and it might even have been the catalyst. But it's definitely not the reason.

CATULLUS. I don't know.

ALI. *(Considers)* Something must have changed recently.

CATULLUS. Yes...

ALI. Do you know what it is?

CATULLUS. Yes.

ALI. Well? Are you going to tell me?

CATULLUS. All right. Jeremiah has AIDS.

ALI. Yes...But we've known that for a while now.

CATULLUS. No. I mean, it's not just HIV anymore. He's dying. Probably in the next couple of years. I haven't any idea how that relates to coming out to my wildly erotophobic little brother.

ALI. Catullus, that makes perfect sense. You know you're going to need the support and understanding of your family, and that support isn't going to be anywhere near secure enough if they think that Jeremiah is just your mentor and if you're terrified of them finding out the truth. You're on the brink of a major personal trial, and you want to know which of your allies are really on your side. I think that's very reasonable.

CATULLUS. Yes, well what I found out is that my allies are decidedly not on my side. I'd rather not figure that out any more.

ALI. Hugs.

CATULLUS. Yes, I know you're on my side.

ALI. But remember it took me a while too. It's not an easy thing to understand. To other people your relationship with Jeremiah just looks like...

CATULLUS. Sexual predation?

ALI. Something like that.

CATULLUS. That's why I'm not coming out. I tested the water, and I've realized that plunging in is liable to induce psychic hypothermia.

ALI. I understand. And I'm not saying you have to have some sort of "coming out" type staged event, but your family *is* going to find out eventually. And I do think that it would be easier for everyone if they heard it from you.

CATULLUS. Yes. I realize that. I don't know. I'll think about it.

* * *

(Back in Toronto, Juvenal finishes putting on his toga and wraps up his conversation with Lydia.)

JUVENAL. Interesting. Very interesting. So, you coming to Saturnalia this year?

LYDIA. You making sacrifices to idols this year?

JUVENAL. You betcha.

LYDIA. Yeah, I think I'm going to decline. We'll pop in after it's over and say hi to everyone.

JUVENAL. You'll miss the symposium. You know you wanna be there for the symposium.

LYDIA. It's so true. But it's probably just an exercise in vain contention anyways. What's it going to be about this year?

JUVENAL. I was thinking it was about time to have one about *Eros*. After all, that's how it began.

[End of Part VIII]

OPENING CEREMONY

(Catullus and Ali arrive at the Kirkman house. Germanicus and Sheila are already there, filling an effigy of Saturn with olive oil. Juvenal has just arrived. Catullus leaves a small gift at the feet of the household gods and joins his siblings.)

JUVENAL. Catullus, Ali. Glad you guys could come out.

CATULLUS. Hello Juvenal.

JUVENAL. Hey little brother, I've been hearing some scandalous rumours about you.

CATULLUS. Oh?

JUVENAL. I was talking to Lydia – You sure you want me to bring this up in public? I could take you aside later.

CATULLUS. I've nothing to hide.

JUVENAL. Brave man. Okay. According to her, not only did you, in violation of Kirkman family policy, attend Perpetua's baptism, but you were observed eating Jesus.

CATULLUS. When in Rome...

JUVENAL. No no no. You're not getting off the hook that easily. No way would Lydia allow your unworthy tongue to profane her holy crackers – unless she had reason to think that you were a "Catholic in good standing."

CATULLUS. I was a Catholic in good standing. It was my niece's baptism. I'm not some kind of reprobate, I made all of the necessary ritual purifications before receiving.

JUVENAL. But you're a pagan.

CATULLUS. ......

GERMANICUS. Juvenal, stop tormenting Catullus and hand me a wash-cloth – there's still some blood on the back of the altar. Someone didn't clean up properly after Opsiconsivia.

(Juvenal obliges.)

JUVENAL. So, did everyone get my message?

GERMANICUS. Yeah. Only I don't understand why I'm arguing in favour of homosexuality.

JUVENAL. I believe that last time you had this argument Catullus was a gentleman and spoke up in support of your girlfriend. I figured you could return the favour so that this time we could hear what he really thinks.

SHEILA. You people are sadistic.

JUVENAL. Yeah, you would think that. That's why you get to be the arbiter. You can help us keep it between the navigational beacons.

(Exeunt.)

(The curtain opens on a Roman style dining room, low table, long couches. The table is laid with a variety of snacks: figs, olives, bread, stuffed dormice, that sort of thing. The four interlocutors take up their positions, Sheila is at the head of the table.)

SHEILA. You know the rules: keep the opening speeches short and to the point, after that you can squabble to your hearts content. If I see any ad hominems or generally bitchy behaviour I'm going to intervene. We've all agreed that, in the spirit of the first Symposium, we aren't going to be drinking tonight. *(She produces 2 gallon jugs of red wine brought up from the Kirkman cellars and places them in the centre of the table.)* But we'd better have this available for anyone who, like Socrates, can hold their liquor without clouding their reason. You've all drawn lots, and I believe that Ali is going first.

(Expectant silence. Ali stands.)

ALI. It's a little hard, because I'm supposed to speak in favour of homosexuality, and I just don't think it's even an issue. I realize that there's a long history associated with this, and that it goes back to certain concerns in ancient cultures, mostly surrounding the idea that somehow a man who engaged in homosexual behaviour would be effeminized by it. Obviously that's just a ridiculous argument in a modern context: we no longer believe that women are naturally inferior to men, and we understand now that gender is a lot more complicated than people used to think it was. I mean, it used to be argued that all kinds of socially constructed gender roles were "natural," even really superficial things like the way that men and women wear their hair. It was considered natural for women to stay at home and do nothing but raise children. It was considered natural for men to exercise dominance over their wives, and even to use violence in order to secure obedience. Within that context, a man who played the "feminine role" in male intercourse was seen as relinquishing his natural privileges and behaving in an unnatural way. Today, we're able to recognize that those "natural" privileges are actually the result of a particular set of heteropatriarchal social arrangements which are inherently abusive, and we've made a lot of progress towards overcoming those male-dominated systems of valuation. We've also made tremendous progress towards understanding that gender is not a simple bipolar phenomenon, it exists on a spectrum, not just within society but within nature. There are people born with androgynous genitalia, people born with male genitalia who later become female, people born with female genitalia but which a masculine brain structure, and a wide variety of other conditions which simply weren't understood in the ancient world. Because we have a more sophisticated understanding of sexuality, and because we have a more egalitarian view of gender, it's only natural that we should shift our thinking about the goodness of homosexual relations. It's not a matter of throwing away the idea of natural moral inclinations, or of the inherent dignity of the person in relation to herself, but rather of recognizing that the way that nature was understood by the ancients was coloured by their social institutions, by their science, and by their cultural assumptions. It's just silly to act as if we haven't made advances in our knowledge, or positive changes in our social relationships when we have, and it's equally silly to insist on some outdated proposition just because it happens to appear to in certain prominent religious and philosophical texts.

(Ali returns to her perch.)

CATULLUS. She says she doesn't know what the issue is. Well I hardly know where to begin. It's bad enough a lot of little limp-wristed mollies congregating in their grotty bathhouses, infecting each other with crabs and scabies and other unmentionable diseases, but nowadays they have to be out of the closet, marching down Queen Street, frightening the children and blocking up traffic. It's disgraceful! They're everywhere. Lecherous old sods ogling adolescent boys in the schools, keeping them back for remedial attention after class. Butch drill-Sargents in far-flung countries with bizarre customs, initiating raw recruits into their disgusting practices. Power-mad sadistic queers clogging up the seminaries and buggering the choir boys --

SHEILA. Point of order.

CATULLUS. It's a disgrace! A perfect disgrace. If I were Jove, I'd have brought out the lightning bolts long ago -

SHEILA. Catullus!

CATULLUS. -- rained down a little brimstone on the Castro. That's what's needed --

SHEILA. Catullus! Shut up! *(There is a brief silence.)* Thank you. I'm sure that we're all enjoying the Monty Python antics --

CATULLUS. Shows you what you know, you great nancy. I'm not doing Monty Python, I'm doing Kenneth Williams.

SHEILA. Well whatever you're doing, your accent is outrageous, and you're not making an argument. If you need a couple of minutes to put together a speech --

CATULLUS. No, no. I can be perfectly serious. Just let me finish this glass of wine. *(He downs it and pours another.)* All right, I'm being serious now: The reason why the contemporary mind finds it so difficult to understand the prohibition on homosexual relations is that we have suffered a complete loss of understanding regarding the purpose of ethical ideals. People today talk about 'morality,' not realizing that this is a rather insipid little notion which arose in the course of the so-called 'Enlightenment' as an attempt to establish a system of conduct based entirely on reason. All of the aesthetic values were stripped from ethical theory, causing it to descend into some trite, reductionistic prohibitions on doing harm to others, and some jingoistic cant about "freedom." Well that's not what ethics is. Ethics is not concerned with the questions like "how can I maximize pleasure and minimize pain for the greatest number" or "how may I act only that maxim by which I might at the same time will that it be a universal law." It is concerned with the question of how I might live The Good Life. It is a practice which is deeply rooted in aesthetics, which involves seeking to produce one's life in accord with coherent stylistic principles in order to make of oneself a masterpiece. Now aesthetic beauty is not arbitrary. It must conform to certain set principles: harmony, symmetry, complementarity, composition, proportion, symbol, archetype. It's not enough for the artist to have lofty intentions. Lofty intentions, when combined with stylistic bankruptcy and lack of discipline can produce nothing but trite, pretentious crap. As in art, so also in sexuality. The proper use of the sexual faculty demands conformity with genuine aesthetic criteria, foremost of which are the complementarity of the sexes, and the creative energies latent in procreative-type acts. Homosexuality is incapable of achieving these criterion. It is a kind of parody of sexuality, an obscene doodle which effaces the truth about the body and renders null its highest creative act.

(Catullus bows elaborately and awaits applause.)

GERMANICUS. All right. I'm going to suggest that the problem with Catullus' exposition of the immorality of homosexual acts is that it assumes that sexual acts, as such, have a singular nature. *Id est*, it assumes that a heterosexual act and a homosexual act share the same fundamentally procreative nature, but that the homosexual act is an unnatural perversion. I'd like to argue that there's no grounds for accepting this thesis. So why do we accept it? First of all, there's a tradition which assumes that the reproductive system has a single natural purpose, that teleologically it is always oriented towards procreation, and all of its parts can only function naturally if they are put towards that end. Obviously this just isn't true. The phallus, for instance, also has a urinary function. There's no question of that being unnatural. So clearly we're faced with a problem, which is that the same human organs can have multiple natural purposes. The sexual function has a procreative purpose, which no one disputes, but arguably it also has the purpose of producing pleasure and relaxation. That's the thesis which Eryximachus defends in the Symposium, and it was widely believed in the ancient world, by many people including the early Stoics, that the use of pleasure in accord with moderation in order to relieve sexual frustration and other forms of tension, was not only natural but necessary in order to maintain interior equilibrium. Which makes sense. For one thing, there's the pretty obvious fact that practically no one can actually limit their sexual release to those occasions when they intend to reproduce, and that if someone does manage to do this they're considered either superhuman or biologically asexual. There's also the fact that in most animals the reproductive system only naturally activates when it's time to reproduce. The rest of the time, birds and dogs all go around enjoying undisturbed freedom from sexual desire, it doesn't bother them, it doesn't wind them up, it's not something that they have to be constantly battling. The fact that human bodies don't work this way should tell us that something different is going on. And the different thing is that human bodies naturally seek out sexual release solely for the sake of pleasure. Now we could follow Plato, and conclude that pleasure is largely bad because it interferes with the action of right reason, but most people won't accept that argument because our natural reaction to pleasure is overwhelmingly to think of it as good. We could also follow Augustine and propose that human nature is somehow inherently distorted as a result of some primeval catastrophe, but that's not natural law, it's just a means of explaining why our natural intuitions and desires are at odds with Christian doctrine. Any reasonable, measured, objective evaluation of the facts, divorced from dogmatic considerations, will come to the conclusion that it is natural and normal to enjoy sex for non-procreative purposes, and that with respect to such usage the gender of one's partner can be rightly considered a matter of indifference.

(Germanicus resumes his post.)

JUVENAL. I'll buy that, Germanicus, but I don't think that the issue with homosexuality has anything to do with whether or not it's procreative. It has to do with what it is. So let's clear away some of the deadwood in this discussion. First of all, lesbianism. Nobody has a serious problem with two ladies going at it, especially if they employ a web-cam so that the rest of us can benefit. People pretend to object just so that they look like they're being rationally consistent. Secondly, the idea that the problem is guys falling in love. The only reason our society is terrified of male love is that it can't properly separate love from sex. In other cultures, male friends could write each other mushy love letters, and kiss, and hold hands in public, and recline on one another's breasts, provided they didn't fuck. That's even in the Bible. Thirdly, the idea that the problem is men engaging in sexual acts together. Listen to comedy, folks: whenever gay sex is being portrayed positively, it's always two guys giving each other blow jobs. Whenever it's being portrayed negatively, it's always anal sex. Why? Because a guy performing fellatio on another guy is no more disgusting than a woman performing it on a man, and anyone who tells you that they find that gross is either a woman, or a liar. The issue is anal sex, specifically anal sex between guys. That's why if you get into these discussions, sooner or later they always come down to AIDS, bathhouse culture, barebacking, BDSM, and all that gay shit, because that's what people are really reacting to.

Now, the gay rights movement is going to tell you that this is "homophobia." I'm going to tell you that it's nature. Does homosexuality exist in the animal world? Damn right it does. Specifically, it is the way that more dominant males express their superiority over submissive males. There are no gay wolves. There are boy wolves who get boned by other boy wolves in the process of the struggle to establish which of them will get the girl wolves. Ditto with every other species that engages in homosexual acts. It is, by nature, a means of establishing who is a player, and who is a loser. That's why all males naturally look with contempt on passive homosexuals, and why all males naturally react with fear to active homosexuals: because we're pack animals. When it comes right down to it we're a bunch of overcomplicated monkeys with delusions of grandeur. And like all monkeys, we look with respect towards the big dadda monkeys who are producing all of the baby monkeys, and we throw coconuts at the sissy little weakling monkeys. And it ain't gonna change, because that's the law of the jungle – the only natural law that's really natural, and actually a law.

SHEILA. Okay. So that's the opening speeches over. Now we can start throwing coconuts at Juvenal.

[End of Part IX]

NOBODY'S ON NOBODY'S SIDE

(Coconuts being unavailable, Ali arms herself with a handful of almonds, deliberating whether she could get away with actually pelting Juvenal with them. There are rumours that the last time the Kirkman boys had a formal debate it ended with Juvenal putting Germanicus through a wall, or visa versa depending on who is telling the story.)

JUVENAL. I'd like to say a few words in my own defence. I'm not saying that gay people are evil, or that God is going to cast **Bolt3** on The Castro. I'm saying that homosexuality is *unnatural*.

ALI. I don't see how something can be unnatural if you admit yourself that it has a clear purpose in nature.

JUVENAL. The word "nature" is kind of the Afghanistan of moral discourse. I'm trying to reclaim it in its full classical glory. When Socrates talks about gay sex being unnatural, he doesn't mean "Icky! Gross. Bad." He means something more like "unhealthy" or "not recommended." Plato turns this on its head in the Laws, but he's pretty explicit about what he's doing, and why he's doing it. He specifically says that he wants to make people feel a sense of gut-level revulsion towards all unproductive sex, the same as they feel about incest, and he explicitly spells out that he wants to use a religious framework in order to achieve this. It's commonly thought that he never managed to find a *polis* that was willing to go along with this strategy...I won't comment on how that relates to the development of Christian doctrine.

CATULLUS. You just did. And your implication is utterly spurious. I'm not denying Plato's influence on the early Christian thinkers, but to suggest that the adoption of a neo-Platonist sexual ethic in late antiquity was a deliberate attempt to control people's sexuality through a system of religious lies is preposterous.

JUVENAL. Sure. You can't deliberately concoct a false religion and foist it on people, 'cause people are ultimately not nearly as stupid as Plato thought. What his ideas needed was a real religion that could credibly support his contentions, which was exactly what Christianity provided.

GERMANICUS. Actually, the most neo-Platonistic sects of Christianity were condemned by the time of the Council of Nicea because they denied the incarnation. Realistically, Manichaeism would have been a better fit for Plato's philosophy.

SHEILA. Time out. You guys are supposed to be arguing about homosexuality, not showing off your knowledge of classical trivia. I think that we should have the discussion framed in such a way that Ali can potentially participate.

ALI. Actually, I was going to point out that Aristotle, Socrates *et alia* understood that their philosophy was for men of a particular social class in a particular political setting. They knew that they weren't philosophizing for the sake of the *barbaroi*, or of women, or of the slaves; that they were proposing a *techne* of the self which would be appropriate for those men responsible for the government of a Hellenic *polis*. I would however like to bemoan the fact that my contribution is given more weight if I invoke certain linguistic status symbols and refer back to a privileged set of Western heteropatriarchal texts.

JUVENAL. Okay, sister comrade, you show me how you're going to arrive at a notion of gay rights without referring to the "privileged heteronormative texts" of the Western canon.

ALI. There are a lot of non-Western societies that actually celebrate homosexual and transgendered persons. It's only because we have a long tradition of homophobia that this is even an issue. If you look at other civilizations, many of them recognize that gay people tend to spiritually sensitive, artistically talented –

JUVENAL. Sure. So your position is that some societies value homosexuals, and that's really great for those societies, and some societies tie them up and throw things at them, and that's fine for them. I've got it now, yeah?

ALI. No...

JUVENAL. Okay. So how do you deal with a society that publicly castrates its gay people or burns them down? Are you going to go in there with your gynocentric homonormative Western privilege and stomp on their heads until they agree to be nice?

ALI. I agree it's a tough question, because you're dealing with a situation where the basic rights of individuals are in conflict with the right to self-determination of sovereign societies. But I think that in those cases, the individuals in question have the right to ask for help from other societies. It's just a matter of extending that help in a way that isn't paternalistic and condescending.

JUVENAL. It's a total pipe dream. Power is the reality. You have the right to talk about individual rights and about offering help only because you have the power to enforce a notion of individual rights which is the direct result of that heteropatriarchal Western tradition that you were whining about earlier. The idea that a person has the right to receive protection from violence inflicted against her by the society in which she lives is an idea which developed out of Aristotle, and Plato, the Gracchi, and Marcus Aurelius, Jesus of Nazareth, Paul of Tarsus, Thomas Aquinas, Immanuel Kant, Voltaire, and Benny Frank. The entire notion of human rights is a Western social construct. The entire notion of self-determining sovereign societies is a Western social construct. You can't get away from it.

GERMANICUS. Look, Juvenal, the point is that none of this suggests, even remotely, that homosexuality is immoral. If contemporary Western culture, as a result of the notion of individual human rights, has arrived at a position of social consensus with regards to homosexual relations which is essentially pro, then I don't see how you can claim that it is valid to enforce a Darwinian notion of heteronormativity based on the psychology of monkeys. So far as I can see, you're very cleverly shooting yourself in the foot.

JUVENAL. My point is that what makes people successful and happy is having the power to control their situation. There can be no such thing as universal human dignity, because dignity – *dignitas* – is conditional on a person's station. Dignity is a measure of the respect that people accord to one another in relation to the degree to which a person has succeeded in securing for himself those goods which are conducive to her happiness. Any practice which helps a person to have that kind of control is virtuous, because that's what virtue is. It's a word derived from *vir,* from the word for a male citizen. Virtue is that which allows a person to procure the privileges which were accorded to citizens and to men in ancient Rome. The homosexual is not virtuous because he cannot dignify himself, he can only become dignified if the rest of society decides to tolerate and affirm him. The actual power continues to reside with those who have the right to grant or withhold tolerance and affirmation. By accepting homosexuality, what we're really doing is establishing power and control over those whom we have designated by the term "homosexual." We place them in the position of having to come to us as supplicants, of having to beg for their dignity as a manifestation of our virtue.

CATULLUS. That is total bullshit. Treating other people with love and respect is not a way of exercising power over them, and needing to be loved and respected is not a manifestation of weakness. This is precisely what's wrong with the entire classical worldview, it's the reason why Christianity spread through the ancient world like wildfire, because someone finally stood up and told the women, and the slaves, and the Jews, that they didn't need to wait for someone to come along and grant them their dignity.

JUVENAL. Sure. If you reconstrue happiness to mean "being eaten by lions for Jesus" anyone can achieve happiness. But I think it's pretty valid to say that most people, given a free choice between being happy by being eaten by lions and being happy by having good food and hot sex, will take the latter. The power of Christianity really derived from the fact that it told people who had never tried to exercise power, people who were at the bottom of the social heap, that they could achieve dignity by being virtuous. The promise that God was on their side allowed them to get over the hump of being scared shitless of defying the existing social order. But it's not really an overturning of classical thought, it's just the application of the insights of classical philosophy to those populations that had been traditionally excluded. Of course all it did was redistribute power throughout social space and redefine "virtue" and "dignity" in such a way that it created new categories of exclusion, like heretics and infidels.

ALI. That's why its important to challenge those categories of exclusion. Because people's identities literally depend on their relationships and on their right to full inclusion within social discourses.

JUVENAL. Racists? Rapists? Republicans? Your philosophy has its categories of exclusion too. All philosophies do, because human beings are fundamentally unable to function in a classless society.

GERMANICUS. What if we just return to the idea that being virtuous is an interior thing, that it has nothing whatever to do with your social status, that it's about your relationship with yourself and with God. I think that solves the problem fairly neatly.

JUVENAL. No way. Your entire conception of what is constituted by the "will of God" is a consequence of your society. Your conception of what a self is is a consequence of your society. It doesn't solve any problem at all, it just creates a little narcissistic bubble in which you can pretend that you're free.

CATULLUS. May I interrupt to point out that no one has even made an attempt yet to answer any of my initial arguments? We seem to be caught in a discussion that assumes that the question of the morality of homosexuality is fundamentally a social question. I proposed it as an archetypal question, a question of beauty and of truth. I agree completely that it ought to be tolerated socially, but that really doesn't address, in any way, the problem of whether it is, or is not, good.

[End of Part X]

ENDGAME

(The stuffed dormice are particularly succulent this year, but the wine is starting to run low. Germanicus recharges his glass. Juvenal adds one to his mental tally. Germanicus has now formally had enough that he can be expected to try double hard to sound like he's still in complete possession of his faculties. Catullus was obviously drinking before the competition even started. Ali's gonna be the tough nut. Lightweight, though. Still on her second glass. Juvenal quietly pours his wine into a potted plant, fakes a drunken wink, and readies his secret weapon.)

GERMANICUS. The reason that no one has answered your original argument is that it's based on a really bizarre paradigm. It assumes that the body has some sort of archetypal significance. I don't see that. It's just a machine, a tool that gets you through the day. Sure, you have to look after it and do basic maintenance if you want it to work for you, and there's kind of an implied obligation "If you have enjoyed the experience of having a body, you will find that yours is supplied with the necessary equipment to provide bodies to others. Please use responsibly." But if you're doing your duty and procreating like you're supposed to, I don't see that it matters what else you use the equipment for. I mean, think of your reason. This is the faculty that leads you towards truth and allows you to know God. But so long as you're doing that, no one makes a fuss if you also use it to play chess or analyze episodes of South Park. So it would seem that if the reason, being the noblest of faculties, may be justly used in the pursuit of trivial pleasures, then surely the baser parts may likewise be used to recreate.

JUVENAL. I can see that Sheila is contemplating how she would feel about being a trivial recreation for Germanicus' baser parts.

GERMANICUS. Come off it. I'm making a serious argument.

CATULLUS. So is Juvenal, and I feel he made it rather well. Sheila would deplore being considered in the manner that you have just described, wouldn't you Sheila?

SHEILA. I would probably demur.

CATULLUS. Because my paradigm is not "bizarre." We all recognize on a deep, psychological level that what occurs when two people have sex is something of far greater significance than a couple of "baser parts" rubbing up against one another and exchanging goo. It has definite aesthetic and moral qualities. Everyone knows that.

ALI. Yes, I agree. But its aesthetic and moral qualities have to do with a relationship, with a sense of responsibility towards another person. I really think that to a large extent all of these ancient moral codes express an anxiety surrounding sex, that the repressions and purifications were really just a way for men to allay guilt feelings. On a fundamental level everyone knows that other people are people, and the sense of conflict that men have traditionally felt around sex is a result of the fact that traditionally, men practised it in a way that was really disrespectful of the personhood of their partners. The horror of homosexuality was a horror of being the one who was disrespected.

SHEILA. Mmm. Like Lady Macbeth washing her hands. Empty ritualistic gestures. I like that.

GERMANICUS. Does that mean our team scores a point?

SHEILA. You're unlikely to score anything else.

GERMANICUS. Maybe a victory greater than that of Hector over Achilles...

CATULLUS. Deviation! Madame Chairperson, he's boasting disgracefully and it's nothing whatever to do with the subject at hand. I think someone had better keep him off the punch. I didn't come all the way out here from North Irving Street to listen to this kind of rubbish.

SHEILA. Have you got a point you'd like to make.

CATULLUS. I do. I would like to address Ali's point. I think it's utterly ridiculous to opine that ancient moral ideas about homosexuality had anything whatsoever to do with the status of women. I know it's *de rigueur* in feminist circles to assume that all social ills are the result of heteropatriarchal oppression, but this really was a discourse that was concerned with the relations between men as men without any reference to women whatsoever. People whose thought is totally wrapped up in postmodern categories might assume that there is a high degree of correlation between our own notions of social life and those of ancient societies, but it's pure illusion. When people in the ancient world "owned" each other, it wasn't a matter of ownership in the modern, capitalist sense. That was considered a perversion of the natural relationships between human beings. A perversion of the natural relationships between a human being and anything, really. The whole ancient concept of ownership was a concept of stewardship. You belonged to another person in the sense that we would speak now of "belonging" in a particular place or a particular group, not in the sense that we would speak of "owning" or "possessing" a thing.

ALI. The ancient world was a society that was really dominated by the fact that economics was based in a culture of slavery, in much the same was that our society is dominated by the fact that economics are based on a culture of mechanization and a theory of unlimited production. I'm not saying that our model is better, I'm just saying that it's obvious if you look at these ancient texts that they are animated by a real, gut-level fear of being dominated, of being enslaved. Even just look at the way that they construe being a sexual being. Your penis is conceived of as a mutinous slave that must be mastered in order to secure your personal freedom and self-dominion. You're telling me that you honestly can't see that that's an obvious symbolic manifestation of guilt and anxiety surrounding the practice of slavery?

JUVENAL. All right, but let's turn that sword the other way round, shall we? What function does the celebration of homosexuality play within a society of mechanization and consumerism? First of all, I think it's pretty obvious that our entire sexual morality is built around the notion that bodies are objects of consumption which we mechanize in order to facilitate their use. We sterilize. We put rubber contraptions on our dongs. We buy little blue pills. We control STIs with drug cocktails. The body is a machine that is expected to produce an output of pleasure when we want pleasure, and babies if we want babies. We treat the body as a possession just as much as the ancients did, just as an individualistic possession rather than as an external possession. That means we self-exploit, self-enslave, and self-abuse in order to produce our own bodies as a consumer commodity. I'm not really sure that's less fucked up.

GERMANICUS. Strictly speaking, the Romans put sheeps intestines on their dongs, drank virility philtres, and dealt with unwanted pregnancies by exposing infants on the highway. But none of that has anything to do with homosexuality. The fact that sex as such has an obvious capacity to become exploitative doesn't speak at all to the question of whether homosexuality, practiced in moderation and with respect for one's personal dignity, is somehow immoral.

CATULLUS. I think the important take-away point here is that sexuality is an area of significant anxiety within any society, because it is intimately connected to the way in which we relate to ourselves, to our own bodies, and to the dignity of other people. Nothing's going to be resolved by playing the *tu quoque* game with some spectre of antiquity. The question we have to ask is: what basic considerations should govern the economics of the sharing of human bodies? My contention is that the criteria of self-possession, reciprocity, integrity, and mutual self-giving have to be central to any genuine moral understanding of sexuality, because those are the criteria for moral relations between people in all spheres of life. And of course I'm arguing that that's not possible in homosexual relations, because the full expression of these goods is...necessarily lacking.

ALI. How?

CATULLUS. Well because it's a closed system. It's just ping-pong. An exchange of gifts always has to be open ended, the gift has to circulate beyond the original givers, otherwise it just ends up stagnating. Sooner or later it devolves into childish arguments about whose "turn" it is, and people start looking for sexual outlets outside of the relationship just to escape from the tedious insularity of it all. The same thing can happen with heterosexuals, but at least they have the possibility of escaping from it through the birth of children.

ALI. Okay, I understand what you're saying. But does that mean that if a heterosexual couple is infertile then they're somehow doomed to this...childish insularity? That they would have to be celibate in order to love one another properly?

CATULLUS. It's a false analogy. An infertile couple marries in the expectation of having children, and generally they see their infertility as a kind of tragedy. It's like in the fairy tales "Year after year, their only sorrow was that they did not have a child of their own." They continue to make love in the hopes that they will be miraculously provided with a happy ending. A gay couple know from moment one that procreation is not going to happen. So to embrace that life they must deliberately enter into the circumstances of a tragedy.

GERMANICUS. This entire argument only makes sense if you assume that anything less than the absolute best is somehow tragic. I'm not arguing that homosexual sex is equivalent to heterosexual sex. Obviously it's not. One of them can make babies, the other can't. That's a pretty big difference.

JUVENAL. Is that "difference" in the sense of "otherness" or "difference" in the sense of "subtraction"?

GERMANICUS. Difference in the colloquial sense. My point was that --

JUVENAL. I can see what your point was, I just thought it was an interesting choice of word, because it illustrates what is really the crux of the whole debate. Because it is a difference in the sense of subtraction. Gay sex is sex minus babies. That's not just a "pretty big difference." It is a serious privation. And I think that you will find, if you consult Thomas Aquinas, who I believe is riffing on Plotinus, that the traditional definition of "evil" rests on the notion that evil does not consist in a thing being of a seperate ontological category of malcreated essences, but rather of a thing being a good which has become threadbare and impoverished to the point of pathos.

ALI. But that's not what evil is. To do evil is to harm another person, to deliberately inflict your will on them in violation of theirs. It's not about deprivations and essences and objective goods. It's about people being able to experience themselves as worthwhile, supported, included, and loved. It's not an abstract thing, and this is the whole problem with the "traditional" approach to evil. It tries to take morality and situate it in some inaccessible realm, whether it's in the inscrutable mind of god, or the abstract realm of forms, or the ocean of the absolute, or whatever. It takes morality out of the human sphere. But morality is human. It's about the acts that human beings commit in relation to other human beings, to whole human persons, including their feelings, and their bodies, and their social relationships, and their subjectivities. The only way to know whether an act is good or not good is to ask people: do you experience good from this, or do you experience harm. Anything else is an act of violence because it takes something which is intimately connected to the personality of the individual and tries to turn it into an object of intellectual appropriation.

JUVENAL. Bullshit. Listen, the reason that you abstract things is not in order to remove them from the individual and appropriate them as a piece of intellectual property. No. You abstract things in order to understand what the underlying logic behind the experience of harm is. It's like...it's like, say you were dealing with some woman who "experienced" being beaten by her partner as an expression of his love for her. You know, "He only beats me because he has my genuine good at heart and he wants me to be a better person." Is this woman expressing a legitimate experience of violence? No. She's been manipulated by some abusive bastard, and the only way to do her genuine good is to appeal to an abstract principle which lies outside of the experience that he's engineered for her. Your theory assumes that somehow people are able to have experiences which don't rely on the fact that other people are exercising power over them, which is naïve to the point of being seriously dangerous. Cute. Charming. Wonderfully innocent. But bloody dangerous. Because it leaves people in the clutches of seriously predatory individuals who are able to construct abusive situations as being in "the best interests" of the person that they are abusing. That's not loving-kindness and respect for another person's subjective experience. It's just abandoning people to their fate and leaving them to fend for themselves when the wolf comes clawing at the door.

ALI. But the issue is, how do you go about helping people without becoming another abuser? I realize that you do get these situations where people have had their self-respect worn down to the point where they're just completely unable to trust in their own judgement. I know that happens, and it's really hard to deal with because there's the risk that you're just going to be the next controlling influence on their life. But I just don't see that with most of the gay people that I know. I see them in real relationships, imperfect, but not abusive relationships in which they genuinely love one another, and where they are able to exercise their own intelligence, and their own judgement, and where the relationships are actually fulfilling and mutual.

JUVENAL. The issue is this: how can a relationship between an old man with AIDS and a boy who was totally vulnerable and isolated possibly be mutually fulfilling? Isn't that the definition of a situation where someone has had their self respect worn down to the point where they are willing to put up with being taken advantage of indefinitely, and where they will see their total self-oblation as being an expression of the depth and authenticity of their love? Because that's what you're standing for, Ali. Sorry. Don't mean to be a bitch about it, but that is what this is about.

CATULLUS. How dare you? How dare you accuse the only person who is even remotely on my side, the only person who has troubled to take the opportunity to sit down and listen to me on my own terms, the only person who actually knows what the hell they are talking about, that they are contributing to my victimization? What gives you the right?

(There is a slight cough from the doorway. Father Kirkman stands there, a platter of Roman delicacies balanced precariously in his hands.)

JEROME KIRKMAN: I'm sorry to interrupt. I know that usually your mother and I would serve you for Saturnalia, but she's put her back out and could use some help in the kitchen. Catullus...

CATULLUS. Yes?

JEROME. I'm going to sacrifice the goat now. Perhaps you would be willing to assist me with the taking of the auspices?

[End of Part XI]

THE DEATH OF THE KING

(A rose-gold pearlescence has gathered on the horizon, spreading across the skirts of the winter clouds as Phoebus Apollo sinks to his rest. A perfect time for the telling of omens. Jerome Kirkman walks towards the slaughterhouse, a weathered outbuilding on the edge of his property. Catullus follows in his father's footsteps, bearing, amongst other things, a slightly chipped clay amphora.)

JEROME. Good weather.

(Catullus surveys the snow-shrouded landscape. The weather is indeed good, but it is inadvisable to assume an auspicious outlook on the basis of pathetic fallacy. Jerome pushes open the slaughterhouse door and Catullus follows him inside. A goat lies in a small pen to one side, reclining on a bed of straw. Catullus put the amphora down atop a simple wooden altar and proceeds to rouse the goat.)

CATULLUS. Wake up. It's time.

(The goat raises its head and looks up, its eyes glazed with the effects of its last supper of red wine and barley. Catullus drapes a garland of winter ivy around its shoulders and crowns it with a wreath of yew. While he prepares the sacrifice, his father builds a fire beneath a large, shallow cast-iron cauldron which is suspended from the ceiling: a remnant of the days when the slaughterhouse was a maple-sugar shack. Once the fire is

built, he takes down a sickle-shaped knife which is hanging on one wall and begins to sharpen it. Catullus lifts the goat in his arms and carries it to the altar.)

JEROME. Would you lead the prayers?

(Catullus scratches the goat's beard a couple of times and places his hand on its head.)

CATULLUS. O mighty god who presided over us in our innocence, veiled possessor of truth, fugitive King driven from his throne by his own sons, we offer to you this sacrifice. Accept it now as we face the crisis of time, the rule of darkness, the passing of the year. Today we turn the world upside down: masters serve their slaves, and fathers their sons, in order to atone for the injustice that was done to you in the beginning of the world. We ask you therefore to bless and receive our offering, restore this wearied world and make all things new.

(Catullus takes the amphora and pours a small stream of water over his father's hands. Jerome strokes the flanks of the sacrifice and guides it down so that it lies still, its neck exposed. Catullus bends over it, covering the eyes of the goat with his arms as he embraces its head, his forehead resting against the brow of the animal. The drugged goat curls its legs quietly beneath itself as the knife slices across its throat. Catullus gathers a bowlful of blood and sets it aside, then helps his father to hoist the animal's carcass upside down into the rafters where it hangs looking strangely reminiscent of Caravaggio's Crucifixion of Peter. They stand together in the cold, watching it bleed.)

CATULLUS. Dad...You heard everything that Juvenal was saying, didn't you?

JEROME. Mmm.

CATULLUS. You mean you already knew. I was afraid you might.

JEROME. I always know everything. You should know that by now.

(Catullus turns away, drawing patterns on the altar. Swirling lines, like miniature galaxies, rise and fall as he traces his finger through the blood.)

CATULLUS. So is there nothing else to say?

JEROME. *(considering)* No... I suppose I would like to ask you why.

CATULLUS. Because I was in love.

JEROME. I'm sorry. I didn't realize you were that desperate for it.

CATULLUS. Why must I have been desperate?

JEROME. You placed your life in danger. You had better have been desperate.

(Catullus returns to his picture. The lines spread out now beyond the boundaries of spilled blood. Jerome takes down a hacksaw, drawing the blade like the bow of a violin across the spine of the goat. The vertebrae split

and the head is slowly removed. He places it on the altar where it gazes with lopsided serenity at Catullus. From the surrounding walls the skulls of sacrifices past look down. They hang their heads now, silently calling the spirit of their fallen comrade to join them.)

CATULLUS. Forgive me.

JEROME. Is that in the imperative, or in the interrogative?

CATULLUS. Please.

(Jerome lays down the saw and contemplates his son for a moment. He says nothing, but takes up a knife and begins to remove the skin of the goat. It falls from the body, revealing mottled pink flesh and curving ribs. Jerome hands the skin to his son who folds it loosely, laying it on the altar next to the head. He lifts the amphora again and washes the blood from his father's hands. As Jerome turns to dry his hands by the fire, Catullus secretly makes the sign of the cross on the side of the hanging carcass. Jerome returns to the altar and studies his son strangely, weighing.)

JEROME. Are you going to take the auspices?

CATULLUS. I suppose. That's what you asked me out here for.

(Jerome hands him the knife and Catullus slowly and deliberately slices open the stomach of the animal. He midwives the organs down into a waiting red wheelbarrow and removes the liver, placing it on the

altar. The firelight shimmers across the dark-red surface of the organ like oil spilled on pavement. Catullus prods it with his finger.)

CATULLUS. It doesn't speak to me. You'd better just consult the books.

JEROME. I'm not interested in what the books say. I want your interpretation.

(Catullus breathes deeply, pulls himself together, prays a private prayer, and then thrusts his hand into the wheelbarrow. Membranes fold themselves around his sleeve like pale balloons. His fingers fumble about in the steaming organs, searching. Eventually they clasp on something hard, clenched tight, still holding on to the remnants of life. He fishes out the heart, its vessels still tenuously connecting it to the body. A slanting ray of moonlight slips through the weathered boards of the building and plays across his bloodied fingers.)

CATULLUS. In the Beginning, it might have been one of two ways. It may be that there was a father, and he was frightened of his son. He tried to destroy his offspring so that they would never be able to defy him, but in time the son rose up, castrated his father and sent him away in disgrace. The son, now frightened by the weight of his guilt, turned on his own children, devouring them in turn so that he would never have to endure his father's fate. But he had brought a curse upon himself which no paranoia could allay. In due time he was deceived, one of his children was secretly spared from his consuming envy, and he too lost his seat upon the throne of heaven.

(Catullus turns the heart over, the straining blood vessels becoming hopelessly tangled.)

CATULLUS. On the other hand, it may be that the father was never really frightened of his son at all, and that the son was jealous and afraid, scared that his father was holding something back from him. It might be that Jove spread the story that his father was a cruel and unjust god so that no one would dare to question his claim to authority. History, after all, is written by the victors. Why not myth?

JEROME. Which do you think it is?

CATULLUS. I wouldn't dare presume to judge the gods.

JEROME. Yes.

(Catullus lays the heart on the altar, cutting away the aorta and the vena cava before placing it in his father's hands.)

CATULLUS. Offer it as a sacrifice and share it amongst your children, in atonement for the enmity which Jove bore to his father, and for the jealousy of Saturn. The rest, *(he gestures towards the remaining innards)* is inscrutable.

(Jerome places the heart on the altar and cuts it open, parting its two halves like a book.)

JEROME. What does it say now?

(As Catullus studies the bisected organ in silence, Jerome takes the remaining innards and places them in the fire as an offering to the gods. The flames flare up to consume the sacrifice, illuminating the shadows of the heart.)

CATULLUS. There is a third possibility. In the Beginning it may be that the father and the son were one, their wills beating in concord like the chambers of the heart. It may be that the father loved the son more than he loved himself, and withheld from him nothing.

JEROME. *(placing his hand on his son's shoulder)* Do you believe that?

CATULLUS. *Credo...* I think.

JEROME. *Ita est.*

(Jerome closes the book of the goat's heart and spears it on the end of his knife. He holds it above the burning organs and its juices run out into the brazier. When it is finished, he gives half of it to his son and they eat together in silence. The eyes of the slain goat, strangely clear, watch them with approval.)

JEROME. Now, I think it's time that we should go up and join the feast.

CATULLUS. *(Washing clean his hands.)* Amen...

[End of Part XII]

civ

Thanatos

Dramatis Personae

JUVENAL, *A brooding bad-ass with a heart of gold. Sort of. Our hero.*

CATULLUS, *His brother, an artist.*

GERMANICUS, *His brother, a stoic.*

GAIUS, *His brother, a ghost.*

CALIGULA (*né* EUSTACE), *Juvenal's best friend.*

BRUTUS, *Bandmate to Juvenal and Caligula.*

JULIA, *Sister to Juvenal and Guardian of Tears.*

A CHORUS OF RAINDROPS

A CHORUS OF SALAMANDERS

A CHORUS OF VULTURES

A CHORUS OF MEMORIES

JUSTICE, *Her eyes gouged out.*

ILLS THAT NEED THE KNIFE

(A road. The night is drawing up her skirts and the moon is peering out from between her thighs. At least that's how Juvenal is thinking about it as he hugs the curves with his thread-bare tires. His brothers, Germanicus and Catullus, are seated respectively in the back and the passenger seats of the pick-up. Juvenal hasn't yet told them where they are going.)

JUVENAL. So I got a question for you guys.

CATULLUS and GERMANICUS. Yes?

JUVENAL. Murder.

CATULLUS. I hate to be pedantic, but "murder" is not a question.

JUVENAL. Is it ever morally justifiable?

GERMANICUS. I'm pretty sure the strict definition of "murder" is unjustifiable homicide.

JUVENAL. Fine, if you're gonna get all tautological on my ass, is homicide ever justifiable?

GERMANICUS. Oh. Obviously.

CATULLUS. I don't think that's obvious at all.

GERMANICUS. What if someone attacks you?

CATULLUS. In the all-too-likely event that one day someone attacks me, I think it improbable that they will be interested in effecting my death. More likely they'll just want to knock me out and steal my shoes. In which case homicide seems rather an overreaction.

GERMANICUS. Okay, what if a knife-wielding homicidal maniac has just stabbed me to death, and then he goes after you. Can Juvenal kill him?

CATULLUS. *(looks at Juvenal)* Please don't. I'll have nightmares about it forever, whereas if I get down on my knees and look sweet and whisper "I forgive you" to my murderer with my dying breath I'll get a free ticket to salvation. Much easier than repenting, in my opinion.

GERMANICUS. You're being deliberately difficult. Take yourself out of the situation. Imagine it with someone else.

CATULLUS. If it's necessary to use force to defend someone, you have a moral obligation to use as little as you must. What's wrong with a shot to leg? If he accidentally kills the man, well, that's excusable because there's no intent.

GERMANICUS. You'd better hope you never end up in a horror movie. You'd leave the serial killer clutching at his wounded leg and then he'd come up behind you and garrotte you with a coat-hanger.

CATULLUS....and I would forgive him with my dying breath.

JUVENAL. Cute. But stupid. Nobody actually believes that you can't shoot someone who's about to rape your sister. And nobody who has ever been in a situation like that believes that you're going to stop and engage in moral deliberation before pumping him full of lead. There's adrenaline, the clock is ticking, she's screaming, and you're reacting on instinct. And your instinct is to pull the trigger, and keep pulling it until the fucker stops twitching. Anyway I'm not interested in arguing about that. I'm interested in premeditated revenge.

GERMANICUS. Uh...okay... can we get a better fix on the nature of the thought experiment?

JUVENAL. Sure. Orestes. Was Athena right to pardon him? Or should he have been served up to the Furies in a white-wine sauce?

CATULLUS. Absolutely not! Red. A Merlot, I think.

GERMANICUS. Orestes did the will of Apollo. You can't argue with the gods.

JUVENAL. Yeah, okay dude, but here's the thing: how do you tell whether it's "the will of the gods," or just the crazy talkin'? Y'know, epistemology has become a little more sophisticated since Aeschylus. We now realize that sometimes when you hear voices in your head saying "Kill the bitch, kill the bitch..." it's not necessarily old *Manticus* whispering in your ear.

GERMANICUS. Good point. I guess that the difference would hinge on whether or not the proposed course of action was in accord with right reason.

CATULLUS. Which in the case of Orestes it clearly was not. I mean...I do think that what he did was utterly excusable. You could easily get him off on a plea of insanity. The man was hounded by horrific hallucinations and in the thrall of maddened grief. But justification...that's a different thing entirely.

GERMANICUS. Okay. So your position is that something which is unjustifiable can be excusable?

CATULLUS. Clearly. To say that something is justifiable is to say that it was right. To say that it is excusable is merely to say that we would all have done the same.

JUVENAL. Yeah. I'm not interested in "excusable." I want to know if vengeance can be just.

CATULLUS. No. It can't. Revenge is a perpetuation of violence which solves nothing.

JUVENAL. So if I kill someone, I shouldn't have to pay?

CATULLUS. Pay whom? The victim has no interest in the matter. An avenger acts out of their own grief. Their own desire for satisfaction. The victim is beyond all that.

JUVENAL. What if they're not? Look, suppose, just for the sake of argument, that the Furies are hugging my ass and they're insistent about this vengeance thing. Suppose that jail is a cake-walk compared to what they've threatened to do to me. Suppose that restless spirits stalk the earth and that the very stones cry out on behalf of the slain. I mean, obviously assume that I'm being overdramatic for effect. But suppose.

CATULLUS. Juvenal, for god's sake, you haven't murdered someone...

JUVENAL. I swear by all the gods, and by the demiurge, and by all the little half-breed bastard gods, that I have not murdered anyone.

GERMANICUS. Good. And you're not going to either. Right?

JUVENAL. You've changed your tune pretty fast, Mr. "Yeah, Obviously."

GERMANICUS. We were talking theoretically then. Probably we're still talking theoretically now, but there's a small risk that you're serious.

JUVENAL. I'm sorry. I thought you believed that theory was serious.

CATULLUS. Juvenal, who precisely are you thinking of killing?

JUVENAL. I'm not necessarily thinking of killing anyone. Maybe I'm just making a point. The point being that I don't want to hear thought-wank. I want the truth.

GERMANICUS. Okay. Well the truth is that retributive justice is permissible, but only when you have a socially sanctioned means of determining whether or not it is actually just. Otherwise you just end up with lynch-mobs.

CATULLUS. And how is a so-called "justice system" different? A posse may well include twelve of a man's peers, and a jury may turn into a bloodthirsty mob. I'm sure you're aware, for example, that a black man is much more likely to face capital punishment than a white man charged with the same crime?

GERMANICUS. So black people should be tried by a jury of other black people, or something equally sensible. *Abusus non tollit usum.*

CATULLUS. *Abusus debet tollere usum* if the abuse is widespread and endemic. What if the accused is a black homeless transwoman with paranoid schizophrenia. Are you going to convene a jury of twelve black, trans, homeless schizophrenics to give her a fair trial?

JUVENAL. Why should a fair trial depend on the jury being sympathetic to the accused? Say some yahoo beats a gay kid to death in the sincere belief that he is saving America from the fate of Sodom. Should he have the right to trial by a jury of Westboro Baptists?

CATULLUS. If this "yahoo" as you call him believes that gay people are a threat to civilization it's unlikely he arrived at that belief of his own accord. Real responsibility lies with the people who taught him to hate, and the people who taught them to hate. Killing him achieves nothing. It just allows society to harmlessly expiate its guilt by slaughtering a scapegoat.

JUVENAL. How is that less true of other forms of punishment?

CATULLUS. Because other forms of punishment allow the guilty to repent, and the victim to forgive. The wrong-doer is offered an experience of compassion, and the victim is ennobled by being granted the opportunity to radically repudiate the logic of hate.

JUVENAL. Repentance and forgiveness are mainstays of Medieval gallows drama. And prison is not an experience of compassion. Think about it: if I told you that a serial killer was going to hang you by the neck would you be more scared or less scared than if I told you that a group of indifferent psychos were going to lock you up for twenty-five years in a ten by six foot box? There's a reason why lifers are routinely deprived of shoelaces.

GERMANICUS. Fear and depression are not objective measures. Statistically speaking, a life sentence is actually only a third of your life. Most people would still have time when they got out. Besides, it's not like you can't do things while you're locked up. In prison you have books. You have your reason, and your free will, and your thoughts, your memories...

CATULLUS. No. Juvenal has a point. Incarceration as it's actually practised is some weird combination of our worst and darkest impulses to torture the guilty for their sins and our noblest desires to see people redeemed. But prison could be turned into an arena of compassion if it included beauty, and reasonable comforts, and opportunities for love.

JUVENAL. Seriously? Cat, if prison were basically a federally funded gravy train I'd be there right now. I'd go and burn down a Walmart or shoot an abortionist or some other public-spirited crime, then sit there eating ice-cream and cozying up to my little maximum security fire-place while Joe tax-payer footed the bill. It'd sure be easier than living out of the back of my pick-up.

CATULLUS. You would not. You'd go crazy within a week.

JUVENAL. Possibly true. So we're back to my original point, which is that capital punishment is not only more just, in terms of the victim, it's also more humane for the accused.

GERMANICUS. Don't be ridiculous. No one believes in capital punishment for humanitarian reasons. I believe in capital punishment because it's a reasonable way for society to deal with people who have consciously, willingly, with malice aforethought, taken it upon themselves to deprive another human being of life. It makes sense because it is proportionate and because it is fair. If you kill someone, your life is forfeit. *Quid pro quo.*

JUVENAL. So what about Orestes? He's way guilty. Conscious. Willing. Premeditated. He openly admits it. But you yourself said that he was doing the will of the gods.

GERMANICUS. Yeah....well, regicide is a special case. Orestes had to act independently; there was no way that he could put Aegisthus and Clytemnestra on trial.

JUVENAL. Okay, so if someone had proof positive that OJ had murdered whatshername, they would be justified in stabbing him in his sleep, yeah? I mean, the justice system having failed.

GERMANICUS. At some point we have to accept that our attempts at justice are poor approximations and let the gods make up the difference.

CATULLUS. Poor approximations which consistently serve the interests of wealth and power. It's exactly the same as the old Roman system where there were different standards for the *honestiores* and the *humiliores*. The only difference is that the Romans were honest about it.

GERMANICUS. Power grants privilege. That's inevitable. But it doesn't mean we can do away with all semblance of justice. The visible punishment of evil performs an incredibly important social function. Yeah, it would suck to be punished unjustly, but if the persecuted innocent dispassionately considers his situation he realizes that human justice is incapable of perfection, and that his suffering is really a necessary contribution to the social order.

CATULLUS. That way atrocities lie!

GERMANICUS. No, because I'm not justifying the misuse of judicial power. The state has an absolute moral obligation to make the laws as just as possible, and an obligation to make every reasonable attempt to apply them justly. All I'm saying is that loosing mere anarchy upon the world in order to avoid the inevitable inequalities that consistently afflict political systems is not a solution.

CATULLUS. So you just shrug your shoulders at human misery and tell the downtrodden that they have a moral obligation to take it like Socrates?

GERMANICUS. No, I'm saying that Socrates, and Solzhenitsyn, and Oscar Wilde and countless other men who have been punished unjustly deserve to be honoured for the contribution their suffering made to society. Also that it happens to be true that those three men, different as they were, all found ways of deriving meaning from persecution.

JUVENAL. I'll be sure to keep this in mind if I ever get thrown in the can. I'll meditate on it deeply then make a Germanicus voodoo doll out of my broccoli and stab it repeatedly with my plastic fork. But don't worry – when your spleen suddenly explodes your suffering will serve an important social function.

GERMANICUS. Okay, Juvenal. You said the murdered have a right to justice. How do you see that happening without taking the risk that an innocent person might be punished by mistake?

JUVENAL. I can't. But consider this: a judge and jury sentence a guy to death, and then go home for dinner. But what if a private citizen undertakes vengeance instead? Don't give me that look. Think about it. Capital punishment, as an exercise of the state is just an invitation to gas the Jews and burn the Queers. Why? Because it costs the executioner nothing. But if someone poked out your eye, and you were reasonably sure that you would lose the other eye if you took revenge...it'd give you pause. Yeah?

CATULLUS. It'd give me pause because pretty much any bastard who wanted to could pin me down and gauge my eyes out with an ice-cream scoop. It would not give a moment's pause to someone who had the strength to slay heaps upon heaps with the jawbone of an ass. In practice, an eye for an eye means 'might is right'.

JUVENAL. Which is why you need the state. A superior force that can pretty much flatten any motherfucker that comes up against it *is* a precondition for justice. I think the state has to have the capacity to lock a man up for life. But the execution of murderers should be reserved to private individuals. 'Cause otherwise, justice is lost and raped.

GERMANICUS. This is one of your stupid arguments. The ones that you make to see if you can get away with convincing other people of batshit craziness that even you don't believe.

JUVENAL. I promise it is not. Please, just try to take me seriously. Say that I witnessed a murder. Say that I have pretty much certain knowledge of who is responsible.

Let's say that the murder was totally unconscionable and that the victim was a child. There's no question of justification. Now I have to decide. Do I kill the person responsible or let them off the hook? And I have to make that decision in the full knowledge that if I take their life I'm liable to spend the rest of my life in a dungeon talking to Brother Roach.

[End of Part I]

BREATH AND SHADOW

A CHORUS of RAINDROPS.

> When on Euphrates' swollen plain
>   First brother struck down brother in his blood
> He cried for us to purge the stain
>   And from the brooding breast of dusky cloud
> As trembling shook the towering pine
>   We scoured the wine-dark liquid from his hands.

> 'Tis always so, for men believe
>   Through water's power their guilt may be absolved
> But every drop we bear conceives
>   A bloody record writ in scrolls of silt
> Each guilt preserved in stony bed
>   Which at the final judgement shall be read.

(The rain spatters the windshield. Juvenal tries to drive it back but the right wiper flaps like a broken wing and the left one leaves long trailing streaks. Through the veil of water, it's hard to see. The pounding on the roof could drive you mad.)

GERMANICUS. Juvenal? Earth to Juvenal. Come in.

JUVENAL. I'm here. I'm listening. I just didn't hear what you said 'cause I'm trying to drive.

GERMANICUS. I was summarizing what I think is your position in rational terms. You seem to be saying that capital punishment is unacceptable because the state will inevitably abuse it. However, the murdered have a right to be avenged. Therefore the best system is to have vigilantes do the killing, and then have the state incarcerate the vigilantes for doing the right thing?

JUVENAL. Something like that. Ideally vengeance would become socially laudable but legally punishable, 'cause then a lot more people would be willing to take it on.

GERMANICUS. So basically you want to turn the legal system into a farce.

JUVENAL. Only if you assume that the purpose of the legal system is to punish wrong-doing. I'm taking the broader view that its purpose is to uphold justice. In my system, the avenger knows that in choosing to perpetrate vengeance he is also choosing to give up the rest of his life. He accepts that justice demands the sacrifice of the innocent. But he also acknowledges that no one can rightly choose to sacrifice an innocent man...unless that man is oneself. So the avenger offers himself up as a holocaust. The legal system doesn't punish him, it simply presides over the offering.

CATULLUS. Does your avenger have any coherent motive? I mean, apart from vague intimations that he's haunted by the Furies or guided by Apollo?

JUVENAL. Sure. Justice. The avenger believes in justice. He serves her and worships her for her own sake. I'm seeing this as kind of a vocation. Definitely not for everyone.

CATULLUS. I see. So only murders that happen to have been witnessed by this self-immolating priesthood of Nemesis can be justifiably avenged?

JUVENAL. The way I figure it is that in the afterlife murdered people wander around wringing their hands and frightening travellers on the road. They linger in hotels and clocktowers, and they wait. What are they waiting for? Justice. But not all of them. Some victims just seem to take it. Like you're not gonna find Seneca moaning in the bath whenever there's a full moon. Or probably sometimes a ghost figures it was a fair cop, they had it coming. Obviously there's no point avenging those deaths. But I'm talking about cases where the murdered one lingers. Where he can't get over it. Where it's not just a matter of abstract principle, but of concrete compassion for a suffering soul. In those cases, my system would create opportunities for redress.

CATULLUS. So you're envisioning kind of a mash-up between Ghostbusters and Unforgiven?

JUVENAL. Can you address my argument rather than just being snarky?

CATULLUS. Certainly. Suppose that ghosts aren't really motivated in the way that you suggest. Suppose the ghosts of the innocent almost invariably move on, and that the ghosts that linger are the ones who can't forgive because they're consumed by wrath and guilt.

JUVENAL. Okay, so when Orestes is goaded on by the memory of Agamemnon --

CATULLUS. A perfect example. Agamemnon slaughters Iphigenia so that he can go off and burn down the neighbours. For ten years he's off slaying Trojans and screwing Cassandra on the side, but he expects Clytemnestra to keep the home-fires burning and her legs closed 'til he gets home. A real piece of work.

GERMANICUS. Uh...guys...can I point out that this argument makes no sense unless ghosts actually exist?

CATULLUS. What do you mean, 'unless ghosts actually exist'? Everyone knows they do.

GERMANICUS. That is patently untrue.

CATULLUS. On the contrary, it is a proven fact. Someone, I can't recall who, did an experiment where people were put in a room with a simple game and were requested to self-report their success. Half of the people were told incidentally that a piece of furniture in the room belonged to a local ghost, and half were not. Those who were told the story did not cheat, those who were not told the story did. The point being that everyone believes in ghosts even those who are too stupid to realize it.

JUVENAL. It's one thing to fear, it's another to believe. I, for example, am scared shitless of god, but I don't believe in him for a second.

CATULLUS. Well, they say "The fear of God is the beginning of wisdom." There may be hope for you yet.

JUVENAL. Don't bet on it. Anyway, if Germanicus will permit me to articulate his position more intelligently and persuasively than he is capable of putting it himself: While it is clear that the experience of ghosts is widespread and common, they might be a purely psychological phenomenon. A projection that combines both the desire for confirmation that there is life after death, and/but/also our subconscious fear that there might be life after death.

CATULLUS. Psychological disorders are remarkably culture-bound, whereas ghosts are reported everywhere and everywhen.

GERMANICUS. Yeah, but the fear of death is pretty transcultural. So is the desire to be able to go on talking to the dead. Plus, different cultures have really distinct ways of imagining that their dead are still alive and of communicating with them. Rome had death masks. Egypt had mummies. Catholics keep relics of the saints.

CATULLUS. There's a massive difference between the commemoration of the dead and ghosts. Ghosts aren't physical. They're felt, or perceived, or talked to entirely on a spiritual plane. People don't make ghosts as a way of easing their grief. They perceive ghosts, and more often than not they're frightened by them.

JUVENAL. You've seen one, I take it?

CATULLUS. Of course. And you, naturally.

GERMANICUS. Hey! This isn't fair. You're excluding me from the argument by appealing to occult knowledge that I can neither verify nor disprove.

CATULLUS. All right, so the next time you make an argument from your experience of "interior equilibrium" can I accuse you of appealing to occult knowledge which I cannot verify? Or would you rather that I simply took you at your word?

GERMANICUS. That's different. Interior equilibrium is a common experience, and strictly speaking I'm not convinced that it's an experience you've never had.

CATULLUS. I'm also referring to a common experience. Everyone agrees that ghosts exist except a skeptical minority. Non-belief in ghosts is just as dogmatic as geocentrism. It only appears otherwise because it's a dogmatic position that happens to be in vogue.

GERMANICUS. Nobody is denying that people experience something that they believe to be "ghosts." The difference is that the heliocentric universe could be confirmed by observable experiment, whereas the nature of ghostly phenomena is completely speculative.

JUVENAL. Alright. I'll give you an experiment. *(Juvenal wheels the car on to a side-road. The wheels churn up gravel. After about a hundred metres he abruptly brakes.)* I believe that I can conjure up a ghost. I believe that it will be sufficient to convince you that they're real. So come on, whata ya say?

[End of Part II]

DEED OF BLOOD

(The Kirkman boys have arrived at a clearing in the woods. Off to one side there is a rock face with a sliver of shadow leading down into darkness. A campfire is lit. Juvenal holds a paper bag in which a bottle of whiskey is concealed. The concealment is unnecessary but aesthetically appealing. Catullus sits next to him, stirring the fire with a stick and watching as the sparks dance upwards towards the stars. Next to the fire is a case of beer from which Germanicus is drinking very seriously, in moderation.)

GERMANICUS. Okay, you've had your drink. Now where's the spook?

JUVENAL. Patience *mi frater*. The time is unripe. Mars isn't in the right relationship to Saturn. There is no murder of crows silhouetted on the tree tops. The moon has yet to turn to blood and the stars have not been torn down. You can't rush these things. Wouldn't be propitious.

GERMANICUS. *(Sighs)* Can we go back to talking about ghosts in the abstract then?

CATULLUS. You mean fruitless squabbling and vain speculation? Well, I'm in.

JUVENAL. Okay, I've got a great fruitless speculation. What kind of ghost would you be? When you pass beyond the veils, and you have nothing to do but smoke ghost smoke and taunt the tourists, how will you conduct yourself?

GERMANICUS. I'm not planning to hang around frightening children. I hope to enjoy the contemplation of the Good, the Beautiful and the True without the distractions and impediments posed by the body.

JUVENAL. Yeah, well say some calamity interrupts your virtuous life and you end up as a ragged alcoholic in a cardboard box and then one day someone knifes you to death for your sleeping bag. You go and present yourself before the Great Tribunal in the sky and they just kind of shake their heads and say you need a bath. So now you're stuck wandering the world in an overcoat that only comes half-way down your forearms and you need to keep busy. What do you do now?

GERMANICUS. A man is not judged by his outward circumstances, but by that which lies within his control. There's nothing about homelessness that should exclude a man from interior freedom and happiness.

CATULLUS. Yes, yes. But how much is anything really in a man's control? So far as I can make out a lot of ghosts are basically good people who simply got too attached to some thing or other. It could be anything. A child. A lover. The taste of apple pie. So they just stay here eternally lamenting their loss. It's terrifying, really, when I think of all that I'm attached to...

JUVENAL. I think being a ghost is just what you do when you're dead. We think it's extraordinary because in the same way that most people are too prissy to cause a commotion in the streets, most ghosts respectfully withdraw into the background because it isn't polite for them to show their faces in an antisupernaturalist society.

CATULLUS. Should I assume that you intend to haunt us when you're dead?

JUVENAL. You'd better hope you predecease me. But Germanicus is screwed. Unless he manages to pick up some good, life-threatening vices before my liver gives out, you and I are sure to beat him to the bottom.

CATULLUS. I don't know. I've always thought that in the race to die of one's sins, Germanicus has a pretty good shot at it.

GERMANICUS. To die? Of what? I rarely drink, I don't smoke, I don't have promiscuous sex, I'm a safe driver, I --

CATULLUS. Yes, yes, you live a dreadfully rational existence. But one of these days you're going to fail, and I'm not sure that you'll survive it. Juvenal might get on to a very cantankerous old age on liver pills, and I may beat the odds, but I think that whenever you decide to make a date with a bathtub and a razor, you're the type who'll have the nerve to go through with it.

GERMANICUS. Okay, firstly, I have failed at many things.

JUVENAL. Name five. And they can't be things like "I fried an egg and failed to keep the two yolks equidistant," or "after three weeks of blue-balls, I finally broke down and had a sly wank in the shower."

GERMANICUS. I deny the allegations. Besides, I shouldn't have to justify the claim that I'm not always perfect.

JUVENAL. Oh come on, don't be a sissy. Prove you're a screw up. You can do it. Here, tuck into the whiskey. Maybe you can do some dangerous driving later on. Want a cigarette? *(He pops a pack of Camel's out of his pocket and in a single motion causes one to shoot out and place itself neatly between his fingers. He offers it to Germanicus.)*

GERMANICUS. And secondly, even if I were to fail at something really significant and important, I would still consider it immoral to take my own life.

JUVENAL. Why? *(He lights the cigarette and smokes, continuing to proffer it to Germanicus between puffs.)*

GERMANICUS. Because it is not in accord with the law of nature that I should divest myself of my body before Providence judges that the time is propitious for me to exit the material sphere.

JUVENAL. But you do believe that this whole mortal coil is kind of a dead-weight that's dragging you down?

GERMANICUS. I believe that the body is an inferior vessel, yes.

JUVENAL. But you also accept the Socratic argument that the gods are your masters and you have to be obedient and do your earthly work like a good boy so you'll get the heavenly doughnut when it's over, yeah?

GERMANICUS. I think any traveller will tell you that they prefer arriving at their destination to being on the boat, but if you jump overboard before you've reached harbour you don't end up on dry land, you just end up drowned. It's not that the gods are arbitrarily forcing me to stay here so that they can extract labour from me with promises of dubious trinkets in another realm, it's that they can see that I have not yet arrived at a safe place to disembark.

JUVENAL. But they have your best interests at heart?

GERMANICUS. It is my experience that Providence is wise and beneficent, if that's what you mean.

JUVENAL. Okay, so Seneca was a failure...and Cato the Younger...and --

GERMANICUS. No. Clearly there are certain circumstances under which a man has reached the end of his life, he is presented only with the choice to die with dignity at his own hand or to suffer an ignominious death at the hands of another, and so he makes the decision to rationally embrace his own death rather than allowing himself to be needlessly debased and humiliated for some tyrant's pleasure. That's not really the same thing as suicide.

JUVENAL. Maybe he would just be debased and humiliated, but wouldn't actually be killed. Caesar was going to let Cato live, by all accounts. Maybe Providence intended that Cato be pushed around a bit and brought down a couple of pegs, and he was wrong to take his life when he did.

GERMANICUS. Maybe. I believe that he attempted to discern his obligations rationally. I wouldn't take it upon myself to assume that I am better able to rationally assess his options than he was.

JUVENAL. That sounds an awful lot like relativism. You mean you can't make an objective determination about a simple question like whether or not suicide is morally licit? 'Cause according to your original argument, it's immoral, but then sometimes it's okay if you're almost about to die anyway, and then suddenly it's a reasonable way of avoiding having to kiss the arse of Great Caesar.

CATULLUS. No, it's very simple, Juvenal. Self-slaughter is *always* immoral, but Germanicus is confused because it's the serious sin that his heroes are most likely to commit. As you've shown, if you allow suicide under any circumstances you will soon find that you are allowing suicide under any circumstances. Or at least under any circumstances where it's likely to occur.

JUVENAL. So you don't allow for suicide at all?

CATULLUS. No. I don't.

JUVENAL. Okay, so if you'd just had all of your fingernails and toenails pulled out, and half of your bones broken, and tomorrow they were going to spit you like a hog and leave you to roast in the noonday sun, and I came in with a nice, merciful draught of poison, you'd refuse it? *(He pretends to add something to the whiskey bottle, and then hands it to his brother.)*

CATULLUS. Oh, no, *(he takes the bottle and downs a very large swallow)* I would say, "Thank you most kindly" -- assuming they'd not cut my tongue out yet – and I would drink your poison to the dregs. But there is a difference between what a man would do and what a man ought to do. Most often a very significant difference. You can't derive morality from the way that people actually behave any more than you can derive aesthetic standards from the way most people draw.

JUVENAL. Okay, so say it isn't you. Say it's Germanicus in the tent, with broken glass stuck up his nose, and you're outside, comfortable, safe, free, and you happen to be in possession of an overdose of morphine. Do you offer it to him?

CATULLUS. Well that's not suicide, that's mercy killing. It's completely different.

JUVENAL. It's aiding and abetting someone else's suicide. It's a basically pro-suicide decision.

CATULLUS. No, it's aiding and abetting someone else's self-determination. It's saying, "In your shoes, I would be weak and do the wrong thing, and it's only fair that I don't demand more of you than I would demand of myself."

GERMANICUS. Hold on, so you're saying that if you think that you might potentially choose evil under extreme circumstances, you should therefore help others commit same evil rather than helping them to do the Good?

CATULLUS. Why should I expect someone else to choose for himself a good that is so manifestly unappealing that I would never choose it for myself? That sort of priggish solicitude is the basis for all moral hypocrisy. It's just too easy to demand heroic sacrifice of others – and ultimately it becomes wholly inhumane.

GERMANICUS. No! People are rarely capable of doing Good without support. A single Legionary is nothing, but surround him with a Legion and he becomes capable of legendary deeds. Sure it's inhumane to demand heroic sacrifice while cowering at home. That's not what I'm suggesting. I'm saying you should come and succor me, and risk sharing my fate, so that together we become capable of a virtue that neither of us could achieve alone.

JUVENAL. Sanctity through peer pressure. Sounds like fun.

GERMANICUS. I'm not talking about pressuring someone to eat their spinach, I'm talking about helping them to live virtuously. The reason it doesn't sound very fun to you is that you think virtue is tedious, and arbitrary.

JUVENAL. No I don't.

GERMANICUS. Yes you do. You make fun of me for it all the time.

JUVENAL. I don't make fun of your virtues. I make fun of you for being an up-tight prick. I mean, look at Catullus. When was the last time that I picked on him for being virtuous?

GERMANICUS. Catullus?

JUVENAL. Yeah. He's loyal. He's patient. He's considerate, and gentle. He's humble. He'll put up with a more of less infinite amount of shit and he's heroically forgiving. I never make fun of him for any of that.

CATULLUS. Thank you.

JUVENAL. See? And he's grateful as well. My problem with people who think that they are virtuous is that they always have some bullshit set of standards that allegedly correspond to an objective fairy-realm of forms. To me, virtue is that which is actually demonstrably good for real human beings, and vice is that which is actually demonstrably bad.

CATULLUS. Yes, but that's not nearly as simple as you suggest. The kind of virtues that irk you really are virtues, just taken out of context. I mean, I should live temperately − I don't − but if I did I would make fewer stupid impulsive choices that are demonstrably bad for people that I love. It's not that temperance is only

cxxxvii

virtuous in the abstract, but that it ceases to be virtuous at all unless it's ordered towards love. The standard isn't bullshit, the problem is that people make of it an idol.

JUVENAL. Okay, let's go back to your claim that suicide is always evil. What if it's ordered towards love? What if I know that I will break under torture and betray my best friend, so I sacrifice myself on his behalf.

CATULLUS. The greater love would be to resist under torture, and maybe survive. I mean, if someone I loved dearly were to kill themselves on my behalf I would feel terrible about it. Not to mention the grief I would feel at their loss. No. The morally superior option, clearly, is to endure with hope. Even in a case such as this, suicide is evil. It's a tragedy. A failure. Though one which I fancy Heaven would excuse.

JUVENAL. Yeah, this is exactly what I'm talking about. All blanket moral assertions ultimately go back to this idea that Somewhere Out There a guy with a set of golden scales is weighing up the hearts of men.

CATULLUS. Yes, I believe that there is a final judgement. I also think it's a perfectly reasonable, likely and defensible probability.

JUVENAL. All right, bro. Bring it.

[End of Part III]

A RIGHTEOUS JUDGEMENT

(Three brothers sit around a campfire drinking whiskey. Germanicus used to be on the beer, but after a certain amount of taunting from Juvenal has consented to imbibe a modicum of rye, not to excess, in accord with right reason. The fire is burning low. The witching hour approaches.)

CATULLUS. All right, but first I challenge you to present an equally compelling alternative. It's too easy to blow holes in other people's beliefs when you haven't any of your own to defend.

JUVENAL. Do you want me to arbitrarily adopt a random position, or would you rather hear what I actually think?

CATULLUS. No thought-wank. Remember?

JUVENAL. Good. In that case, I think there are three serious possibilities. One: you float around in Tartarus and slowly forget your entire life until you turn into a shade. Two: nada, kaput, like the Buddha's candle. Three: if you've been good you get to eat Philly and strum harps for all eternity and if you've been naughty a snake bites your bum. Forever.

GERMANICUS. What about the transmigration of souls?

JUVENAL. Fuck the transmigration of souls. Reincarnation is just one of the other three options with a coda.

CATULLUS. Straw man.

JUVENAL. Do you have something better to propose? Because as I recall your brilliant theory was that people ended up as ghosts fannying about because they were too attached to life to "move on." Can I assume that when they "move on" they "go towards the light"?

CATULLUS. Ridicule is not an argument. You haven't demonstrated that Heaven and Hell are unconvincing propositions, merely that your understanding of them is superficial.

JUVENAL. Look, the only people that they let in there are folks who never boozed, never slept around, never played loud music, never smashed anyone's face in, never fucking lived. It's like Socrates says, "If you just live as though you're dead, then when death comes you'll be perfectly happy and content to contemplate ethical propositions and the nature of substances forever and ever amen." Basically, the idea here is that the afterlife is interminably boring but if you're a sufficiently boring person you'll think it's great.

GERMANICUS. Okay, first of all Socrates was not a boring person. He was one of the greatest human beings that ever lived, and it was generally agreed that he was wise, that he was --

JUVENAL. An insufferable gadfly who deserved to be put to death for getting underfoot. Aristophanes thought he was a bore, and the Athenian court determined that he was criminally irritating. Sorry, but my ideal of permanent happiness does not include being asked persistently dumb questions by a sexually frustrated gay man in a toga.

CATULLUS. You don't believe a word that you're saying, you're just trying to get up our noses. I can see by the look on Germanicus' face that he's raring to take the bait, but I will not. You know perfectly well that all the best accounts of the afterlife involve an awful lot of very colourful characters being redeemed by the clemency of the gods. I believe the foremost exponent of the doctrine said something about the Prostitutes and the Publicans getting in ahead of the insufferably smug. You're just setting up a straw-man because you're terrified of the Final Judgement.

JUVENAL. Don't psychoanalyze me. I'm perfectly content to consider the possibility of a final judgement, provided someone can present me with some kind of reasonably fair criterion by which a life could be judged. So far as I can tell the criteria usually put forward basically amount to "Did you follow the arbitrary rules? Were you a member of the club? Do you know the secret handshake? Did you do the silly dance? Have you had the magic bath?"

GERMANICUS. I can see several possibilities for how men could be fairly judged. First, you could get the opinions of all of the people who actually knew the person, put the evidence forward, and take a vote, like with Orestes. Second, you could allow the person to judge himself: did he live up to his own standards, looking back at his own life, is he happy with how he lived? Third, there could be a reasonable and objective set of standards for what makes a good human being. The religious and moral proscriptions of each particular culture would likely be a rough approximation of those standards, and obviously a man, through the exercise of right reason and of virtue, would be able to come to understand which of his culturally inherited ideals were more or less in accord with truth and which were socially constructed.

CATULLUS. The first one is frankly dreadful. I refuse to believe that the gods could possibly have so constructed the universe that our final role within the panoply of Creation would be determined by a macrocosmic popularity contest.

JUVENAL. The argument from "I refuse to live in a crap universe" is a dumb-ass argument.

CATULLUS. "Beauty is truth, truth beauty." And if it's not, I'll have no truck with it.

GERMANICUS. Okay, okay. Obviously option one would have to include some fine-tuning, like, people would have to see each other as they truly were and then evaluate. Or maybe only those who were virtuous would get a vote.

JUVENAL. You mean that someone, presumably the gods, would force the popular assembly to vote in accord with objective standards? How is that different from your third possibility?

GERMANICUS. Maybe it's not. Okay, so what if you judged yourself by your own standards. You would see your life as it really was, you would see what you had accomplished, who you had helped, who you had hurt, what kind of mark you had made on posterity, and then you would decide whether you had lived well or not. That sounds reasonable.

CATULLUS. It sounds perfectly terrifying. Any man faced with the truth about himself, deprived of his flimsy excuses, confronted with the pettiness of his motivations and the paltriness of his loves could only possibly deliver a single verdict. *(He does the Roman emperor thumb down thing.)*

JUVENAL. So you're saying that you think you would condemn yourself to hell?

CATULLUS. My actual plan is to throw myself prostrate and grovel piteously before whatever gods happen to be present.

GERMANICUS. Why don't you just live in a manner that you wouldn't be ashamed of?

CATULLUS. Why, he says, do I not simply swallow the moon? Germanicus, everyone does utterly shameful things all the time. Just some people realize it when they're fifteen and others don't figure it out until they're eighty. I imagine that there are some who don't come to the knowledge of their own inadequacy until the moment of death. It must be a *terrible* shock.

JUVENAL. Yeah, okay, so human beings are morons. It is written. The sages nod their agreement. And so does the guy at the end of the bar. And yes, Germanicus, "human beings" includes Socrates. It even, shock horror! includes you.

GERMANICUS. Look, obviously hubris is a serious spiritual ailment and the man who imagines that he is just and virtuous is often overcome with pride. I'm not ignorant of that basic truth. What I'm saying is...there's a way of living in order to become the kind of person who is well prepared for happiness in the world to come. There's a way of ordering your life and ordering your soul that is in accord with nature, with the formal perfection proper to a man, and with the will of the God. So if death relieves us of our bodies and brings us closer to the perfection of spiritual reality, then a spiritual way of living is a kind of preparation for the soul in the same way that developing lungs and sucking your thumb *in utero* is a preparation for birth. Clearly nobody is ever purely spiritual in this life, not even Socrates, but I think it's reasonable to propose that some people are well enough prepared that they're able to survive the transition from this life to the next without losing their identity or going crazy.

JUVENAL. So we're back at the notion of an eternal summer camp for the virtuous and the dull.

CATULLUS. Only if you imagine that the "formal perfection proper to a man" is a perfection based entirely on criteria of reason and virtue. If God is an artist instead of a moral mathematician it would be a completely different scenario. Heaven would be the ultimate ecstasy, the opportunity to savour, to contemplate eternally the handiwork of the greatest Master that ever existed. It wouldn't be eternal indifference, interior equilibrium and endless satisfaction with the contemplation of one's own detachment from all created things. It would be a sort of rapture, a permanent state of divine madness, like prophecy, or poetry, drunkenness, or orgasmic bliss, but without the silliness, and the angst, the hangovers and the awkward mornings-after. It would be...like watching one's own small performance in the greatest opera ever composed, seeing the great masterwork in which you were privileged to play a role and rejoicing with the whole company together.

JUVENAL. I am definitely sympathetic to the idea of a triumphal cast party that goes on forever. That would certainly be cool. It just seems like the kind of thing that would be way too cool to be likely. In my experience of life, nothing that good ever actually pans out. It always looks like paradise on the postcard, but when you get there it's bedbugs and malaria and fifty-year old strippers who steal your passport.

CATULLUS. Yes, but if you make of your life a masterpiece and then it turns out that death is nothing more than the eternal memory of your own life, or endless drifting through nothingness, or simply "kaput" as you put it, what have you lost? To live beautifully is to live fully, so you might as well.

JUVENAL. *(Finishes the whiskey with a sigh)* I think it's obvious where this will go. We'll get into that same old argument about objective moral standards and criteria of judgement, only instead it'll be about objective aesthetic standards and criteria of adjudication. I'm not sure I want to go there and I think the moon has just collided with Sirius in a very auspicious way, so the time is upon us.

GERMANICUS. Actually, Sirius is over there, you can't see it because of that tree.

(Juvenal picks up a pack from the ground and slings it across his shoulders. The moonlight falls over a crack in the rock face behind him. From the fireside it just looks like a shadow, but it opens wide enough to admit a man. Germanicus and Catullus linger at the campsite, slowly putting out the fire, picking up litter, avoiding the inevitable. When not a spark remains, they reluctantly follow Juvenal. One by one, the shadow swallows them. They descend.)

[End of Part IV]

DIRGES AND CANTICLES

(Underground. A Chorus of Salamanders clings to the walls, their bodies white and blind. The beam of the flashlight disturbs their vestigial eyes causing them to flee into the crevices. It creates the suggestion that the caves are haunted by beings that disappear on sight.)

GERMANICUS. *(Breathing shallowly, clinging to the flashlight with white hands.)* Uh, how much further does this go on?

JUVENAL. Not far. Why, are you scared?

CATULLUS. He's claustrophobic, you know that. You should have set this up outside.

JUVENAL. Not possible. You can't just open up a portal to the cthonian realms in a parking lot. You have to look for the deep places in the earth where the shadows flicker between this world and the next. Holy places. Like this. *(He swings his flashlight in a large arc, revealing that they've just emerged onto a ledge. In the cavern below a waterfall descends, shrouding the cave walls with a plume of mist. Stalactites reach down towards the stream, and the walls glisten with mottled colour.)* Isn't it fantastic?

CATULLUS. It's lovely. But it's so far down.

JUVENAL. It's like less than ten feet. Don't be a wuss.

CATULLUS. Juvenal, you know perfectly well that Germanicus hyperventilates in closed spaces, and that I get vertigo if I wear platform shoes. It is a beautiful location, I admit that. But you went to a lot of trouble to make it look as though our coming here was random, a natural development in the argument, when clearly it was planned. And I can't help feeling you might have planned it more considerately.

GERMANICUS. I assumed it was just a normal exercise in Juvenalian schadenfreude.

JUVENAL. You people have no faith in me. Fear is important. There's a reason why sacrifice is potent, why the descent of the gods is so often described by the imagery of rape, why Paul says you're s'pposed to work out your salvation in fear and trembling. Fear makes you alert, it activates your spiritual senses and makes you open to things that you don't expect to see.

GERMANICUS. You mean it overexcites your imagination and makes you more susceptible to auto-suggestion.

CATULLUS. It does both. That's why you can make carnival tricks that mimic supernatural experience. But the fakeries are transparent to anyone who's experienced the real thing. *(He steps a little closer to the edge, whitens, and pulls back.)* Germanicus, you seem happy to be out of the tunnels. Why don't you go first? *(He waits until his younger brother has dropped out of earshot, then whispers.)* Which is this?

JUVENAL. The real thing. What do you think?

CATULLUS. I was afraid that you'd say that. I sort of hoped that you were just toying with Germanicus to make a point. Who are you planning to contact?

JUVENAL. Gaius. Why? Are you afraid of ghosts?

CATULLUS. No. I morally object to necromancy.

JUVENAL. I think you morally object to drops of more than a metre. But prove me wrong. I'll be happy to argue this with you at the bottom. *(He descends.)*

(The ritual space has been prepared in advance. A small stone altar has been erected next to the pool, circled by bamboo torches. As Germanicus lights them Juvenal bends over the pool, holding a strange device. It looks sort of like a metal strainer, but semi-precious stones have been bound to it with wire.)

JUVENAL. Hey little dudes, where are your mommas?

A CHORUS of UNHATCHED SALAMANDERS.

We swim alone.

JUVENAL. Abandoned, yeah? Not for long. *(He lowers the device into the water, strains out a clump of amber-coloured eggs. Like a hundred eyes glistening in the torch-light, they look up at him expectantly.)*

CHORUS.

Why do you take us from our waters?

JUVENAL. To die.

GERMANICUS. Uh, Juvenal, who are you talking to?

JUVENAL. The salamander eggs.

GERMANICUS. Cool. What are they for?

JUVENAL. According to legend, salamanders are semi-mythic creatures, offspring of fire living between the worlds. They're amphibians in a double sense, inhabiting this living realm but also capable of surviving in the waters of the Styx.

GERMANICUS. Uh huh. According to legend, salamanders can also put out fires with the frigidity of their bodies. And I believe Leonardo da Vinci wrote that they have no digestive systems. Both of which are demonstrably not facts.

CATULLUS. *(Arriving, slightly pale and out of breath.)* The great confusion of scientific materialism is the assumption that when the spiritual qualities of a being are described they are a mistaken description of its physical characteristics.

GERMANICUS. Okay, what do you mean by "spiritual qualities" in this case. I would use that term to refer to the parts of a human person, or a divine being, that exceed the merely physical. Reason, conscience, volition, that sort of thing. But in the case of a salamander, its supposedly supernatural powers are pretty obviously just fanciful explanations for mundane facts. Like, salamanders like to hide out under piles of rotting wood, so if you put old wood on your fire salamanders might come streaming out. Also, if you put wet, mouldy fuel on your fire, it might go out. Ergo, salamanders are elemental creatures born in fire and they have the power to extinguish it with their bodies.

CATULLUS. The spiritual characteristics of animals, plants and inanimate things are at least partly a product of their interaction with human imagination. They acquire significance, and over time that significance becomes invested in the creature. By perceiving, naming, and narrativizing the natural world we alter it. The problem with the scientific paradigm is that it sees the natural world as a *fait accompli* which men simply observe and describe, not as a masterwork in which we are co-creators.

GERMANICUS. So you're saying that whenever some ignorant peasant makes up a story, that story becomes real?

CATULLUS. Absolutely. And I've even heard rumour that sometimes the lofty theories of scholars have become real as well. Though I shudder to believe it. I doubt that academics are suited to such power.

(As Catullus and Germanicus bicker, Juvenal produces a strange object from his back-pack. It's the size and shape of a child's stuffed animal, but its body is wrapped in old bandages and elastic bands. It wears a human mask, painted in a childish hand, with the tattered ears of a teddy-bear sticking out above it. He places it overlooking the altar.)

JUVENAL. He's exaggerating to irritate you, just so you know. But he is onto something. It's not so much that if you make shit up, it's true, as that if a group of people come together and formulate a concept that concept becomes real. I don't mean that in some airy-fairy sense, I mean that it becomes meaningful within that group, and that the meaning is potentially transferable to other contexts. So, for example, we have a somewhat arbitrary concept of "apple" that includes Ida Reds and Granny Smiths, but not quinces and pears, and if I utter the extremely arbitrary pair of syllables: "a-pul," it really has the power to actually summon forth out of your psyche a whole series of images, meanings, and associations. The fact that these concepts have demonstrable power, in terms of their real effects on the behaviours and perceptions of human beings is not contestable.

GERMANICUS. Right. But you want to summon a ghost, and presumably you think that the ghost in question is something more than a social construct.

JUVENAL. I'm saying that the identity of a human being *is* socially constructed. Our souls are produced by the mechanism of relationship. I would not be the same person if I hadn't been named after my stillborn older brother *(he gestures towards the strange masked creature perched above the altar.)* Or if my parents hadn't decided to raise me like a Roman. Or if either of you two had never born. Etc. Etc. Who I am and who I know are inextricable. So. I think it follows that the part of a human being that persists after the body is gone must exist within a world where reality itself is defined by the products of relationships – or of society, which is really just relationship writ large. A world of concepts, as opposed to material objects. Basically, Plato was nearly right except that he thought the Forms were pre-existing objects that defined human perception, whereas actually they are the lasting products of human consciousness.

CATULLUS. Then why are you planning to try to contact the spirit of someone who never had a single social interaction in his life. Gaius died before he was even born. If what you're saying is true, he shouldn't have a soul at all.

JUVENAL. Wrong. As soon as a person's existence is known of by other human beings, that person exists within a realm of human relationships. A soul is not just individual experience, it's the whole of a person's identity. Gaius has a relationship with our mother, for example. She believes that he was conceived by Mars in a golden shower, or that he was Hercules' dog in a past life, or whatever crazy thing she thinks, and that's part of who he is. Her belief that I am a kind of inferior substitute for him is part of his identity. As is the fact that I made a new body for him by filling my teddy-bear with earth from his grave when I was nine. And that I have carried it with me as the sole permanent feature of my life for over fifteen years.

CATULLUS. And all of these are excellent reasons why you should not be trying to summon Gaius, of all people, from the dead.

JUVENAL. I think they are excellent reasons why I should. I need someone on the other side that I know well, that I have a relationship with, and that I can trust.

CATULLUS. Juvenal, do you remember when Mom used to have those death masks of her parents that she terrorized us with?

JUVENAL. *(sarcastically)* No. I'd forgotten about it completely. That's why it's a recurring motif in half of my songs.

CATULLUS. Well this is precisely the same thing.

JUVENAL. No! It is absolutely different. For one thing, Gaius is innocent whereas Grandpa Maidenoak was a flagitious fuck. For another, keeping relics and communicating with the ancestors is not bad in and of itself. You'd never tell Germanicus off for wearing Grandpa Kirkman's sweaters. What made that particular instance evil is that the masks were used to shame and intimidate us into thinking that we were letting down posterity if we behaved like normal kids.

GERMANICUS. Hold on a sec. First of all, it's not like those masks were a constant, or even a regular feature of our childhood. They were trotted out like maybe once a year. And I always understood that the point of them was to teach us reverence for our ancestors. It was a way of making posterity present so that we would understand ourselves as being part of a larger system and to create a sense of continuity between this life and the next. Not so that you would be scared that Grandpa was going to disown you if you put cockroaches in Julia's bed.

CATULLUS. Lines were crossed. You don't remember, because you were six. In any case, my point is that when you try to bring the dead into the present, you provide them with the means of living again vicariously through you. The boundary is set on a life for a reason, through the wisdom of the gods and the dead have no right to meddle in the affairs of the living.

JUVENAL. If I was planning to ask Gaius "O Gaius, I am lost and confused in the wilderness of my existence. Please usurp my self-determination that I may be certain of my path," or "I seek knowledge of the future. Will my next beer run succeed? Or will all my empties fall, shattering, and slice my toes off? Tell me, O wise one, for I fear to risk any enterprise unless I have foreknowledge of success," then yeah. You'd be right. But in this case I'm looking for information that is properly within the purview of the dead, and I'm not planning to make a habit of it.

CATULLUS. Whether you're planning to make a habit of it or not is irrelevant, because the information that you're looking for has the capacity to exercise decisive control over the rest of your life.

GERMANICUS. When did he say that?

CATULLUS. He's trying to work out whether or not to commit a murder. Haven't you been paying attention?

GERMANICUS. Oh.

JUVENAL. Let me put it this way, Cat. You're assuming that I'm consulting Gaius so that I can get the final confirmation that will push me over the edge. Actually, I'm consulting Gaius in the hopes that I will learn something that gets me off the hook.

CATULLUS. Why don't you just actually lay out the situation and consult with us? You know us well, we have a relationship, and you can trust us absolutely. Neither of us is going to run off and report you to the police, and neither of us possesses the necessary means to thwart you if you decide to ignore our advice.

JUVENAL. Because neither of you can tell me whether there is, in fact, a soul in agony, whose blood cries out from the stones to be avenged. I've already received your counsel, I appreciate it and I am actually going to think very seriously about everything you've said. But I also need information and that you can't provide.

CATULLUS. Then why are we down here? Why involve us in this?

JUVENAL. Because I need witnesses. I need to know that whatever answers I get, they're real and not just my imagination dicking me around.

CATULLUS. You should know better than to think that's going to work.

JUVENAL. I suspect I know what you're going to say and we don't have time to argue about it. Timing is important, and the hour is at hand. Either you're going to stand by me, even though you think what I'm doing is dangerous and stupid, or you're going to turn your back and abandon me. Just tell me which it is.

CATULLUS. Obviously I'll stay, but I'm not participating. I'm only here to provide triage if it comes to that.

JUVENAL. Thank you. *(He picks up the salamander eggs, singing to them softly.)* Hushaby. Don't you cry. Go to sleep my little babies. *(The Chorus quivers silently, running circles in their jellied orbs. Juvenal slowly lowers the eggs over the flame. As they cook, the delicate membranes burst. The torches flicker. Juvenal begins to intone the Homeric hymn to Hermes. His voice is musically trained, now rising in a triumphal cadence, now falling to a guttural lament. The Greek words echo down the walls of the cave, calling forth the salamanders who stand in silent witness while their children are born by fire into death.)*

[End of Part V]

TRANSPORTS OF MADNESS AND TERROR

(An eerie light breaks on the shadows of the deep. Mother salamanders stir in the depths of the pool, waiting for their children to return from the other side. From across an infinite divide, there is the sense of something approaching, something formless and void. The witching hour has come.)

CHORUS of SALAMANDERS.

> Gaius. Gaius.
>   We call you.
> Come up from the waters,
>   Child unborn.
> Born by fire
>   By fire we die.
> Come up to us
>   Your brother calls.

GAIUS. *(looks across the divide towards his brothers.)* Yes?

GERMANICUS. *(feels as though the torch-light has fragmented into a Mandelbrot fractal based on an image of a child's cloudless eye. He feels slightly sick but resists the inclination to faint.)* Uh, Juvenal? Are you going to ask your question?

JUVENAL. Ask who?

GERMANICUS. No one. Nevermind. *(He closes his eyes. Takes a deep breath. Clears his mind. Opens his eyes. The ghost is still there, wavering in the torch flame, a formless form, somehow suggestive of a boy.)*

JUVENAL. If you can see it, tell him I need to know about Numa. Is he at peace?

GERMANICUS. Who the hell is Numa?

JUVENAL. Gaius will know what I mean. Just ask.

GAIUS. *(The voice is surprisingly clear, childlike, matter-of-fact.)* I don't know. I can find out. Stay. Wait.

(The torch-flame sputters and goes out. The plume of mist rising from the surface of the pool sweeps across the cave like a cloud. The ghost is gone, but the void remains. Germanicus sits down cross-legged and massages the bridge of his nose.)

GERMANICUS. He says wait. He can find out. But...

JUVENAL. But what?

GERMANICUS. I don't know, Juvenal. I don't know what I saw.

JUVENAL: I said that I was summoning a ghost. You saw something that behaved like a ghost. What were you expecting? Bed-sheets that moan?

GERMANICUS. I was... I don't know. Catullus, did you see anything or am I just hallucinating?

CATULLUS. I don't see the need for triage yet.

GERMANICUS. Guys, seriously. This isn't like we're having a séance for fun because we're fourteen years old and have suddenly turned into girls. Let's say that this spirit, or whatever, comes back and says "No. Numa is not at peace. His soul cries out to be avenged." And let's say that I'm the only one who hears that, but I faithfully relate what I have heard. And then Juvenal kills someone. And then it turns out that there's some kind of undocumented neurotoxin in salamander eggs, and I happen to be susceptible, and this is only happening in my head. You see my problem?

CATULLUS. So do what I'm doing. Refuse to participate.

JUVENAL. Fuck you Catullus. This isn't a game. I haven't had a proper night's sleep in over a year. There is something that is destroying me, and I don't really care whether it's actually "objectively" a ghost, or whether it's some kind of deep-seated subconscious impulse, or whether I was secretly kidnapped by the CIA and conditioned with murderous suggestions. All I want is to know what I have to do to placate it so I can get my life back.

CATULLUS. Whatever happened to the disinterested worship of Justice for Justice' sake?

GERMANICUS. Yeah. Seriously, Juvenal. If the problem here is that you're basically crazy, then the problem is that you're basically crazy. That's not going to be fixed by murdering someone.

JUVENAL. Yeah, I'm not stupid. Obviously the entire problem might boil down to "I have schizophrenia." That's why you're here, because if your hallucinations corroborate my hallucinations then it maybe stops being reasonable to typify them as "hallucinations," yeah? I'm trying to do the kind of responsible fact-checking that I would hope anyone would do before committing to a grave, life-altering course of action. But I can't do that unless you give an honest, straight-forward account of what you're experiencing. An account. Data. Not an epistemological meta-analysis of your account.

GERMANICUS. No. That isn't fair. There's too much riding on it... And I'm not even sure that if there is a ghost that it has the right to demand bloody vengeance.

JUVENAL. Do you acknowledge that it might have the power to inflict suffering if it doesn't get its way?

GERMANICUS. I guess.

JUVENAL. Look at yourself. You're visibly trembling. You look like you're going to be sick. You're holding yourself together and resorting to philosophical speculation to try to distract yourself from the fact that you are scared shitless. And all you've experienced is a tiny glimpse into the otherworld, a brief exchange with a fairly benign spirit. Are you telling me that if that ghost, or a bigger, meaner ghost decided to relentlessly haunt you that would not constitute suffering?

GERMANICUS. What I'm saying is it's better to suffer evil than to do it.

JUVENAL. I'm not talking about doing evil. I'm talking about putting things right. I'm talking about justice.

CATULLUS. You're talking about compounding injustice. You don't have authority over life and death Juvenal, and if you seize it you will not find peace. Nor will that innocent spirit. If someone is haunting you, then they are in the wrong and they will gain nothing by being impatient for vengeance. You're committing yourself to the perpetuation of your own suffering for the sake of a spirit that would be better served by helping it to forgive.

JUVENAL. It's not up to you. You're not participating, remember?

GERMANICUS. No, but if you want me to be your go-between you're going to answer Catullus' objection.

JUVENAL. Okay. Forgiveness is a beautiful thing, I'm not going to deny that, but Catullus you yourself made the point that if you demand heroic virtue of another person you very quickly become callous to their pain. If someone has just been raped, you don't tell them that they have a moral obligation to forgive their rapist. Maybe they'll choose to do that, and if they do, wonderful, but if they don't? It's not fair to go piling up moral demands on someone who is already faced with unendurable suffering.

CATULLUS. It's not a matter of piling up moral demands. It's a matter of refusing to participate in an evil that won't actually bring the sufferer any relief from his suffering. I believe that this ghost might sincerely imagine that simply watching their murderer suffer and die will make them get over the grief of losing their life. But it won't.

JUVENAL. What makes you think that? 'Cause it runs completely contrary to the natural moral instinct of the vast majority of human beings.

CATULLUS. When Achilles drags the body of Hector behind his chariot, his grief for Patroclus is not quelled. Neither is he motivated by any "natural moral instinct," he's motivated by rage.

JUVENAL. So you don't believe that there's any such thing as righteous anger?

CATULLUS. I didn't say that. I just don't think that righteous anger expresses itself in vengeance. It expresses itself in a desire to bring about positive, constructive change not in a desire to inflict fruitless counter-destruction on the enemy.

JUVENAL. So you're saying that when the family of someone who has been killed say that they feel sick because the murderer has been let off on a technicality, that's because they're experiencing a perversion of the thirst for justice, and when they say that they feel relief at the murderer's execution that relief is disordered?

CATULLUS. I don't know anyone who has actually been in that situation, and I doubt that you do either so lets talk about things that we can substantiate from our own experience. I do have the experience of being hurt, sometimes of being hurt quite badly by other people. I have the experience of being terribly spiteful and I also have the experience of forgiving. The former invariably feels wonderful at the time. It's like you're on top of the world, and the power and the dignity which were stripped from you are restored as you stride atop the broken body of your enemy and throw your head back and laugh with sheer exhileration. And afterwards either you feel afraid, or you feel guilty, or you become paranoid about being judged for similar offences in your own life, or you just feel empty. Whereas when you forgive it's very difficult up front, but then it's over and you're able to actually be at peace.

JUVENAL. Okay, well my experience is to the contrary. I've had the experience of just letting things go, of trying to forgive and move on, and I've also had the experience of giving back what I got. I mean, maybe I just really suck at forgiveness but whenever I've tried it I've found that it leaves it me feeling really powerless and if I actually have to be in the same room as the person that I've forgiven it's like this angry little beaver is chewing up my guts and desperately trying to build a dam out of them to keep me from exploding. Whereas if someone really pisses me off, and then I beat on them, and they beat on me, by the end of the night we're black and blue and reconciled. Or if they don't want to reconcile, then at least it's over. The debt has been settled, and I can walk away from it. And honestly, if I take down someone who has it coming I don't lie awake at night stressing about it.

CATULLUS. It never occurs to you that one day you might be the one who has it coming?

JUVENAL. Sooner or later God'll cut me down, sooner or later gonna ... cut me down. Of course it's occurred to me, primarily in the context of other people settling the score. Like Germanicus here. Why do you think I never beat him up? I only tease him. Why? Because one night I pushed him too far, and afterwards he came out with a notebook containing full documentation of every single time that I ever flicked his ears, or stepped on his head, or socked him in the gut since he was like five years old. So he waited until I was drunk, and he hog tied me, and then he waited until I'd sobered up and he went over the accounts. He was really rational about it, and very clear about how fair it was. After I got over being mad and plotting vengeance I realized that actually I didn't want to escalate the situation, and that I'd deserved everything I got. So now we're cool.

CATULLUS. Because one: you're crazy, and two: you love him. If one of your direst and oldest enemies did the same, you'd be on him with a posse. You wouldn't in a million years recognize the legitimacy of his claims, and therefore you wouldn't recognize his right to take revenge. Besides, if everyone who you had ever harmed in your life got together and took it out on you, and eye for an eye, you'd be a badly mangled pile of loosely associated organs joined together by bits of lightly sauteed skin.

JUVENAL. Maybe. Maybe that's what I deserve.

CATULLUS. Of course it's what you deserve. There's no maybe about it.

JUVENAL. Fine, but that's not what I'm talking about. Obviously in order for vengeance to be just it can't just be getting back at people because you were hurt. In like 99% of cases, there's guilt on both sides. That's why forgiveness is in order. It's like "You screwed me out of five bucks!" "Yeah, well you screwed me out of two beers, and you know what those two beers were worth? Two-fifty each." The account is not actually unbalanced, or if it is unbalanced it's small change. What I'm talking about is a situation in which the victim is completely innocent, where there is a clear and unambiguous debt left unpaid.

CATULLUS. Like Iphigenia?

JUVENAL. Yeah, sure.

CATULLUS. So Clytemnestra was in the right when she slayed Agamemnon?

JUVENAL. Well, I mean --

CATULLUS. And therefore, we must conclude, Orestes was punishing his mother for settling up his father's account. So Orestes was definitely in the wrong. Or was he avenging poor innocent Electra? Or punishing his mother for adultery? Only it seems that matricide is a rather steep price for taking another man to one's bed after being abandoned for ten years, and what precisely is the proportionate punishment for reducing one's daughter to the status of a slave? No. It won't do. As soon as you try to work out guilt and innocence, who owes whom and how much, you immediately find that all the accounts have been in arrears ever since Pandora opened her vicious little box. The lines are hopelessly tangled and none but the gods could sort them out. And may I point out, incidentally, that when Athena is finally called in she rules in favour of clemency? It is forgiveness, and not vengeance, that finally lifts the curse from Tantalus' line.

GERMANICUS. Okay. Okay. Both of you shut up. I've heard what you have to say. Let me think. *(He assumes a vaguely yogic posture, eyes closed, and retreats into his own head. Speaking silently, he continues the conversation without Juvenal or Catullus.)* Gaius, what do you think?

GAIUS. *(Looks out from one of the parapets of Germanicus' interior fortress. Here he is much more easily visible, much more normal looking than out there in the cave with the scent of burnt eggs and the smoke of lamp oil lingering in the air. He looks like a child, with a mop of toffee-coloured hair like Juvenal's, and a very quizzical expression.)* I think you should tell Juvenal the truth.

GERMANICUS. You mean do the right thing, regardless of the fact that I know it will probably have negative consequences? Yeah. Probably that's right.

GAIUS. Juvenal will be alright. He always is.

GERMANICUS. Do you know who he's thinking of killing?

GAIUS. Yes. I know.

GERMANICUS. Who?

GAIUS. He'll be angry with me if I tell you.

GERMANICUS. I think you should tell the truth. Regardless of whether or not Juvenal will be angry.

GAIUS. It isn't up to me to say. I won't lie to you. I just won't tell you. You have to ask Juvenal.

GERMANICUS. Okay. Do you know the answer to his question?

GAIUS. Yes. I have it now.

GERMANICUS. And?

(The ghost climbs up so that he's sitting atop the ramparts, he leans in close and whispers in Germanicus' ear. Germanicus nods, remains sitting for a few moments, opens his eyes.)

GERMANICUS. All right. I've decided. I'm offering you an exchange. I know the answer to your question, and I'll give it to you under one condition: I want to know who you're planning to kill.

JUVENAL. Sorry. But there's only one answer you could have gotten where offering me that deal would make sense. If you'd been told that Numa sleeps peacefully, and that all I need are some powerful antipsychotics to calm me down, you'd have just told me. The fact that you're bargaining means that he lies uneasy in his hidden grave but that you entertain some hope of being able to prevent me from avenging his death. I appreciate the sentiment, but you've basically just told me what I need to know.

(Juvenal extinguishes the remaining torch, blows out the lamp. Silence and darkness fall.)

[End of Part VI]

TALES OF HORROR HAVE THEIR USE

(Backstage. The show is still several hours away, but there's plenty of work to do setting up. Catullus enters carrying a large bouquet of black irises and a Georgia O'Keeffe style ram's skull. Caligula tinkers with his "drum set," an organized miscellany of found objects like corrugated roofing and a rusted engine block. Juvenal is stressing over which shade of lipstick will make him look less like a drag queen and more like a corpse.)

JUVENAL. We're doing the Sabbath cover tonight, second song before the end of the set. It's not negotiable.

CALIGULA. I hate that song. Why can't we do "Stargazer"?

JUVENAL. Because my Ozzy is better than my Dio, and we haven't figured out a way to make it work with stand-up bass and that pile of junk.

CATULLUS. Also, when Juvenal does his tormented scream from the pits of Hell, Rob Halford gets a hard-on.

CALIGULA. Maybe. But my problem with "Black Sabbath" is that it's thinly disguised propaganda for the Christian idea of hell.

CATULLUS. Hell isn't a necessarily Christian concept. As I recall, the Greeks invented some rather ingenious tortures for the wicked and I never got the impression that Tantalus would one day be reprieved.

CALIGULA. So the Greeks had the same propaganda. So what?

CATULLUS. So, the punishment of evil is not propaganda. It's a widely apprehended truth.

CALIGULA. The punishment of evil, sure. I'm all for that. What I have a problem with is lying to people, making them believe that if they do wrong they are going to boil forever in a lake of flame.

CATULLUS. It's an image, it's not meant literally. Like in *Inferno*, no one believes that Dante was giving a literal description of the contents of hell. He was developing an allegory to show the effects of evil on the soul.

CALIGULA. But the premise of this song is not "if you do evil, it will corrupt you. You will hurt others and harm yourself." The premise is that Satan walks the earth strewing destruction and dragging souls to everlasting fire. It's not about the effects of evil on the soul, it's about how there's an eternal bogey-man lurking in your closet to drag you down to Hell.

CATULLUS. Caligula, I don't understand how you think you can play heavy metal if you're not prepared to deal with the fact that half of it is about man's final option. Why do you think I'm decking the stage with skulls and funeral flowers? The entire genre is basically *memento mori* for the postmodern age.

JUVENAL. That and giant electric lizards on motorcycles.

CALIGULA. I don't speak Latin. Remember?

JUVENAL. *Memento mori:* Reminder of death. Basically it's a long-standing popular art-form that directs people's attention towards their own mortality as a moral exercise.

CALIGULA. To me this sounds morbid, not moral. Not that I object to morbid, but they are different things.

JUVENAL. No they're not. You can't think about moral questions without thinking about what consequences your actions might have, and death is, one way or another, the summation of all consequences.

CALIGULA. No. Death is the end of all consequences. Once a person is dead that's it. If you don't punish them before they die, they will not be punished. That's why heaven and hell were invented, like Santa Clause, to frighten people into being good, because otherwise they will reduce morality to "don't get caught."

JUVENAL. So what's your objection? If stories of heaven and hell have the social effect of causing people to basically police themselves, why is that bad? 'Cause, yeah, I think basically you're right. If I think I can get away with something, probably I'll do it. But if I believed that I was going to have to lug rocks up a hill for the rest of forever while some one-eyed monster whipped me with a spiked tentacle, probably I'd think twice.

CALIGULA. Exactly. The problem is that when you make morality a fairy-story, only simple men believe it. It means that smart and powerful men can make up moral stories to suit their purposes, while ordinary people are crushed beneath a yoke of shame. It's like the story of Cinderella, which is also a lie. It makes poor girls dream that whenever a man in a fancy car picks them up at the club, he is going to take them away to a fairy castle and make their problems go away. So then they spread their legs. Only religious stories make brown people afraid that if they defy the white men's rules, they will burn in flames. They force prostitutes to work in the dark, underground, in poverty where nobody cares if they are killed or abused. They make slaves obedient to their masters, and women obedient to men who beat them every night. You tell me, who is benefiting from these stories? Morality? Or power?

CATULLUS. But the most articulate proponent of the heaven and hell thesis said that those men were going to hell, and that the prostitutes and the tax-collectors would be clutched to the Father's bosom, dressed in rich robes and given a fatted calf.

CALIGULA. Because Jesus told the truth. Don't think I'm not down with Jesus. He was a little loco maybe, or maybe just people who wrote it down didn't understand the things he said. But he was my brother, my compadre, and he died for me. So I don't trash talk Jesus. What I'm talking about is religion, and that's a different thing.

CATULLUS. But Eustace, what on earth is the point of Him dying for you if there's no Hell for him to save you from?

CALIGULA. He died to show that we do not have to be afraid of men in power. He died to show that there is freedom in death, so that the people who were being oppressed by Caiaphas and Pontius Pilate would not be afraid to claim their dignity. This is paradise, when men live as human beings, when they take responsibility, and make amends when they do wrong, when they work together in brotherhood, and when they are not afraid that their lives are ruled by unseen spirits full of wrath.

CATULLUS. But the success of this "paradise" was always predicated on the belief that if I died for righteousness sake I would win eternal peace. Pagan Rome did not enslave people through an appeal to everlasting punishment. It enslaved people with an appeal to the *gladius hispaniensis,* the strength of the Legions, and the terror of the cross. The Roman gods were not served because they would subject you to everlasting fire or give you eternal joy, they were served because they would give you success in battle or a good harvest; because they would blight your love life or afflict you with boils if you let them down. In the Roman world, ordinary souls just went to the Lethe and floated forever on the waters of forgetfulness. Only the mighty were important enough to be tortured for their sins, or privileged enough to raised among the gods. The dignity of the ordinary person was not achieved through materialism. It was achieved by offering the humble and the meek the opportunity to inherit an everlasting Kingdom.

JUVENAL. Yeah, but guys, social good has no necessary connection to objective reality. It may be true that a tremendous amount of good was done by promising the poor that they would receive eternal victory in the mead-halls of the Lord. It may be equally true that evil was perpetuated by telling people that worms would feast forever on their brains if they defied their feudal masters. None of that has anything to do with the objective existence of heaven or of hell. There are plenty of fictions that are morally convenient, and there are plenty of facts that are really kind of shit.

CALIGULA. Yeah, like Santa Claus. Parents want their children to be good, so they make up a story about a man in a red suit who can always tell if you've been naughty or nice. Then Christmas comes and they put on a show to make the kids think Santa really exists. But he doesn't. We know this. It's the same thing with church. They want you to be good, so they make up a story about a man in the clouds who is all seeing and all knowing, a father who can't be fooled. Then they put on a show every Sunday to make it look like he exists. The only difference is that with Santa Claus the promises are small. The parents can give the kids the things that Santa promised. With religion, your pastor can't give you heaven. All he can give are promises that can't be verified until it's too late.

CATULLUS. You've completely missed the point. Santa Claus, and the Easter Bunny, and even the story about the lovely grey-haired man on his throne above the clouds, they're fictions. Of course they are. But fiction isn't the same as a lie. A fiction is an attempt to translate a deep and mysterious intuition into words and images that can be understood. St. Paul tells us this explicitly: the truth about heaven is that "eye has not seen, nor ear heard". We believe these stories because they strike a chord at the heart of our being, because we are attuned to that music, because they awaken us like a bride at the sound of the bridegroom's step beyond the door.

CALIGULA. When you say it is a mystery, what you mean is that you haven't seen it, you haven't heard it, you haven't tasted it. It's never showed up on a radar screen. And no one else has seen it either. That is the definition of something we don't know. This is the problem. Faith is just wishful thinking. It is "the substance of things hoped for, the evidence of things not seen." Hebrews 11:1. Like I used to know an old woman, and she was sure she was going to win the lottery. She used to tell me, "Today, I'm going to win." I say "How do you know?" She say, "I had a dream." But she never wins. She spends so much time thinking about winning, imagining what to do if she wins, that to her it becomes real. This is what prayer is. The "remembrance of last things." It is day-dreaming about heaven until heaven becomes real to you.

CATULLUS. The difference is that if the old woman steps back, and looks at her situation, she'll realize that she's throwing money away and that it's very unlikely that she'll ever get it back. Heaven is not that way. It's not just a promise of eternal sunlight, and endless mirth. It's a promise that there will be eternal justice, and divine forgiveness. That the soul is immortal, that human beings are free, that beauty is absolute and that my life matters. If your old woman stops buying lottery tickets, she gets back the money that she's spending. But if I give up on heaven what exactly do I gain?

CALIGULA. You gain control of your own life. You gain freedom from shame. You get to live as if this life matters, and you get to act as though you are just as important as other people.

CATULLUS. I think you're exposure to religion has been unfortunate, and I'm not going to pretend that it's uncommon. Still, it's a mistake. It's like...like when an American president uses the word "democracy" to mean US aggression towards strategically valuable foreign countries. People living under US occupation, voting for puppet governments, may think democracy highly overrated – but they've never actually experienced it. It's the same with faith. Clearly there are people who twist religion to their own advantage. Clearly there are people who use it as a way of gaining control over other people, as a way of building themselves up by making others feel ashamed, as a way of exploiting the vulnerable. But those are misuses of religion, not religion itself.

CALIGULA. Then why is it that the abuses are so much commoner than "religion itself"?

CATULLUS. Can you think of a single good where that isn't the case? Love, for example. The word is invoked all the time to get gullible people into bed, or to guilt-trip one's children, or to sell overpriced chocolate. It is everywhere abused, and yet so priceless that we're willing to put up with the abuses in order to sip from its cup. Or freedom. I can hardly think of a single evil that hasn't been committed in its name. But who can live without it? Religion is the same. It places you in control of your life, and then secures your freedom by investing it with meaning. It delivers you from shame, and then helps you to live in a way that you would not be ashamed of. It says that this life matters, because it is the arena in which you achieve the identity that you will carry with you beyond the stars. And it says that you are absolutely valuable, absolutely equal, because you are the beloved child of the divine. So again I ask, what is to be gained by abandoning belief?

JUVENAL. Reality.

CATULLUS. If I find a deeper significance in the stanzas of a poem, I do not thereby lose the literal meaning of the words. On the contrary, I regain them. Faith does not divorce me from reality, it readies me to deal with it.

JUVENAL. That sounds very nice when you're arranging flowers and talking in the abstract, but in *reality* you are not equipped to deal with life. Your grasp of the real world is tenuous at best, you consistently make ridiculous choices on the basis of absurd beliefs, and you aren't in control of anything.

CATULLUS. Well, that might be fair. But the same could be said of you.

JUVENAL. *(in a sing-song tone) Tu quoque, tu quoque...*

CATULLUS. Besides, I've always been that way. It's not like I used to be a thoroughly rational, sound-minded, sensible person until one day I found God and went off the deep-end.

JUVENAL. No, but here's my point. In theory, the Christian religion is all about setting people free. Free from guilt, and sin, the fear of death, enslavement to the passions, the tyranny of lust and the wiles of the world. But in reality, how do you gain that freedom? By renunciation. By mortification. By death to self. By submission to the will of God. By taking up your Cross. The picture on the brochure is real nice, but as soon as you get down to the fine print you realize that what it actually means is: you can't have good sex, you can't drink very much, you can't party, you can't swear, you have to spend an hour every Sunday morning listening to some boring crank tell you what you're doing wrong, *and* you have to pretend to like Christian rock. As soon as you think about what sin actually entails, you realize that "freedom from sin" is like offering a kid freedom from swimming pools and ice cream.

CATULLUS. Oh yes, Juvenal. In your embrace of sin, you gain such lovely freedoms. You're free to live in the back of your pick-up truck, to get blind drunk and fuck ugly women, to spend your Sunday morning stumbling around hungover trying to scrounge enough cigarette butts from the grocery store parking lot to roll yourself a smoke. You're free to alienate people by treating them like crap, and you're free to go hungry so that you can afford enough whiskey to pass out before you paranoid delusions manifest and demand a debt of blood. Where do I sign up?

JUVENAL. How about on the page where you have to actually do some of the things that your faith demands of you? You're just like that old woman, except that you're crazy enough to think that you're gonna win the lottery without buying the fucking ticket.

CALIGULA. Which is fine. If you want to be religious, but you don't actually do anything, why not? It brings you comfort. Okay. You don't force it on other people. Good. I have no problem with that. It's still fantasy, but it's harmless.

CATULLUS. But that's not --

(The door opens. A young man enters, clean-cut, average height, with Asian features and glasses. He carries a stand-up bass, and looks like he probably teaches middle-school children how to squeak through Pomp and Circumstance for a living. Juvenal has renamed him after the noble Roman Family responsible for the overthrow of Tarquin and the death of Caesar.)

BRUTUS. Did I miss sound-check?

JUVENAL. Nah. The guy was supposed to be here fifteen minutes ago. If he's not here in an hour I'll start to freak. Sit down and grab a beer.

CATULLUS. *(hopefully)* You don't, perchance, believe in life after death?

BRUTUS. What a strange question. No. I don't believe at all. I know.

[End of Part VII]

OUT OF A DIM VEIL

(Tonight is a big deal and in spite of his purported sangfroid, Juvenal is visibly on edge. He keeps rolling an unlit cigarette like a baton around his fingers. His phone buzzes, and he checks the messages: Germanicus says Julia's flight has been delayed and she might not make the show.)

CALIGULA. What do you mean you "know"?

BRUTUS. I mean I've seen it.

CATULLUS. Really? What did it look like?

BRUTUS. *(looks embarrassed and uncomfortable.)* I've never talked about it with anyone. It was a long time ago, when I was a kid. My little sister and I were in a car accident. She was killed and I almost died. When I woke up in the hospital I remembered seeing her go. She was running ahead of me, and calling me to come and follow her. Umm. She was very excited and she kept telling me to hurry up because there was so much to see. We came to a river and I said that I didn't think we should cross it, but then she said "I'm already on the other side." I could see her there, and I could see that she was happy. That's all.

JUVENAL. Okay. How upset are you going to be if I try to deconstruct that experience?

BRUTUS. Why would I be upset?

JUVENAL. Because obviously it's very personal, and really important to you, and usually when someone has just shared something private they don't want to hear it ripped apart. What I'm saying is feel really free to tell me to back off, because your feelings are a lot more important to me than winning a stupid argument with my brother.

CATULLUS. Excuse me, I'm looking for my brother Juvenal. Have you seen him anywhere?

JUVENAL. What? I'm just being considerate.

BRUTUS. I don't mind. If you want to question my experience, I'm not going to be threatened by that.

JUVENAL. Okay. So basically you had a near-death experience, and because of that experience you believe in some kind of afterlife. Yeah?

BRUTUS. Juvenal, you've never been to the Philippines, but you've sailed along the coast right? So basically you had a near-Philippine experience, and because of that experience you believe in Manila. Yeah?

JUVENAL. Cute, but not a good analogy. The existence of the Philippines isn't controversial because a country is a category of thing that we know to exist, and generally adding something new to a pre-existing mental category is a less fraught enterprise than adding a new mental category

BRUTUS. Why should immaterial phenomena be a new mental category? All mental experience is immaterial. Consciousness. Free will. We don't have a compelling material explanation for those things, and yet we experience them daily.

JUVENAL. You're basically proposing a "god of the gaps" type theory. We don't know how consciousness could emerge out of a purely material system, but we do know that purely physical effects can cause loss of consciousness. Ditto for volition. There are well documented forms of brain damage that cause people to completely lose their impulse control and basically lose their free will. Both of those facts suggest that we're looking at phenomena that arise out of biochemical, or bioelectric systems and that those faculties are dependent on the functioning of those systems. Which does not bode well for the survival of consciousness after death.

CATULLUS. I thought you believed in ghosts.

JUVENAL. Yeah, well not for the purposes of this particular argument.

CALIGULA. Juvenal is right, even if he doesn't believe what he is saying. Near death experiences have been debunked by science. I'm sorry, I don't mean to piss on your sacred calf. I believe that your experience is important, I just don't believe that it's proof of life after death.

BRUTUS. I assume you're referring to loss of proprioception under ketamine sedation and NDE-type experiences reported by fighter pilots at extreme speeds?

CALIGULA. Yeah. That's right. I saw a doctor talking about it, how a lot of near-death experiences are happening in cardiac units because when a patient flat-lines then the doctors have to start working on them before they're fully sedated, or they have to use low levels of sedation because the patient is too weak. Basically, all that happens is that a person who has no experience of doing drugs gets high in the OR.

BRUTUS. But I had no way of knowing that my sister was dead. She was in a different ambulance from me, and she died on the way to the hospital. I know that sometimes when a person is unconscious they are still perceiving things and sometimes the brain will put things into a dream that it perceives out of the waking world. But I can't think of a reason why anyone would have told me that my sister was dead.

JUVENAL. They might have mentioned it. Ambulance dispatch. Or if they were talking to your parents outside of the OR. There's a hundred different ways that you might have overheard. From there, yeah, when a person experiences trauma the psyche creates whatever it needs to allow you to get through. That's why someone stuck on a mountainside with a broken leg might dream that they're home with their family having a turkey dinner. The subconscious is some powerful shit.

CATULLUS. I suppose that might explain why someone with a serious axe to grind might start having hallucinations of weeping ghosts and fire-eyed furies. The id might be casting around for a reason to avenge its own injuries, and start using that immense power to compel the unfortunate ego towards violence.

JUVENAL. Ha ha. Cheap shot. But I already established that I was aware of that possibility, so no score.

CATULLUS. You do realize that Germanicus is incredibly suggestible? Far more suggestible than he would like to believe?

BRUTUS. Has the subject of conversation changed?

CATULLUS. No, not at all. Private aside. I was actually just about to leap to your defence, to point out that this entire line of argumentation seems to be predicated on the notion that material experiences are somehow eminently reliable whereas spiritual experiences are suspect. I think it's stupid. Take your example about how people with brain damage sometimes experience a reduction of volition. No they don't. They experience a reduction of effective volition. If you grab my arm and start forcibly hitting me in the head with my own hand, I will experience a loss of voluntary control over my arm. That has absolutely no bearing on my free will, it's just a material limitation. And as for consciousness, there's plenty of evidence that consciousness persists in people who are in comas, in people who are in vegetative states, in people who are "unconscious," and of course in people who are asleep. All of which is absolutely consistent with the theory that free will and consciousness are immaterial realities which exist in some sort of tenuous relationship with the world of matter.

CALIGULA. It's not stupid because I know that the physical world exists. If I run into a wall, it hurts. Simple.

JUVENAL. Uh, don't go down that road buddy. Catullus will have you for breakfast.

CALIGULA. How?

JUVENAL. Because you don't actually know that the material world exists. No one has known that since Immanuel Kant and the devil sat down to breakfast. All that you actually know is that you have sensations, and you believe those sensations to be located in a thing that you call a body. But actually your entire relationship with your body is really just a series of sensations which you perceive to be mediating a series of so-called "external" sensations. You have no means of fact-checking those against an objective standard.

CALIGULA. If I am having a sensation of sticking my fist in your gut, I can easily verify that it is real by seeing if you have a sensation of having my fist in your gut.

JUVENAL. Come on, Little Boot, I know you can do this. No one tell him what the problem with his argument is. Let him figure it out for himself.

CALIGULA. *(looks like he might very well perform the above-mentioned experiment.)* You're going to say that I only know that you exist because I have sensations of seeing you, hearing you, feeling you, smelling you.

JUVENAL. Basically, your argument is right. Even if we assume that the other minds problem is boring, and that solipsism is for losers, we're still stuck with the fact that you and I are sitting around comparing sensations which neither of us can objectively verify. It's not really that different from Brutus and Catullus sitting around comparing notes on their respective spiritual experiences, and any minute now one of them is going to chime in to point out that people who have near-death experiences describe a remarkably similar set of phenomena.

CATULLUS. I was actually going to chime in to point out that in the contest between spiritual experience and material experience, spiritual experience is the more persistent and reliable of the two. If your body is unconscious, and you're dreaming, you're aware of yourself but you're neither aware of your body nor necessarily limited by it. Your primary experience is an experience of being, of self, of awareness, of freedom, of purpose. All sensation is contingent on the primary experiences of spiritual existence that we call "consciousness," but the perception of spiritual existence is not contingent on material sensation.

CALIGULA. That's not true. Your earliest memories, what are they memories of? Sensations. What are you conscious of in your dreams? Colour. Textures. Emotions. Sounds. To be conscious is to be aware of some sensation. We have no other kind of experience. You're trying to confuse things by turning them upside down. Like a dream, we know is just chemicals in the brain imitating sensation. No one thinks the things they see on LSD are real. No one thinks the things they see in dreams are real. Maybe I can't form a fancy argument to prove you wrong, but I can tell when someone is twisting everything to make it look like black is white. I'm not stupid.

CATULLUS. I agree that you're not stupid, but I do think that you're wrong. Your LSD example is a perfect illustration of precisely the opposite point. A lot of people on LSD perceive their experiences to be absolutely real and think that until you've done hard hallucinogens you're living inside the matrix. In their defense, great art is practically impossible unless you can acheive an abnormal state of consciousness. And even in science, all of the really big break-throughs require a paradigm shift – and more than a few scientists have acheived that using substances that we consider "hallucinogenic." Francis Crick comes to mind. It's the same with dreams. The belief that our dream-lives are just the random epiphenomena of rapid-eye movement is an extremely modern belief, and not even a very widespread one. Most people, including respected psychologists, believe that dream experience is tremendously relevant to waking life. Dream interpretation has been practised in every culture across the globe. I'm not turning everything "upside down" as you say; modern skepticism has turned everything upside down. Materialism is not "obviously true," it's a complete inversion of mankind's most natural intuitions.

CALIGULA. You mean humankind's most natural superstitions.

BRUTUS. May I interrupt? I'd like to ask Eustace a question?

CALIGULA. Go ahead.

BRUTUS. It seems to me that the best evidence that we could possibly find to support the idea of life after death would consist of contact with spirits, or experiences like mine. We have millions of witnesses who have experienced these things. Can you suggest another kind of evidence that you think would be better?

CALIGULA. If a ghost, or a near-death experience, caused a person to know something that they actually couldn't possibly know otherwise, then I would be convinced.

BRUTUS. That happens all the time, but it's very difficult to prove to someone who chooses disbelief. Skeptics can always find an infinite supply of obvious cranks who are easily debunked, and this produces the illusion that the real cases are actually just cranks who haven't been debunked yet.

CALIGULA. So why can't these "real cases" be scientifically demonstrated?

BRUTUS. Because real cases are rarely repeatable. Scientific inquiry requires reliable, repeatable data that can be replicated under laboratory conditions.

CALIGULA. That's exactly what makes me suspicious. If this is a real thing, why should it be so hard to make it happen?

BRUTUS. Because we aren't meant to live as though we're on the other side. Seeing the other side has helped me to understand my purpose and to live well, but sometimes it happens that after an experience a person becomes obsessed with death, either with talking to the dead, or with trying to get back to the threshold between worlds, and that's very unhealthy. The true thing about everything that you're saying, is that we are meant to live in this reality as though it were real, because the illusions of the world can prepare us to be without illusion.

CALIGULA. What you're saying is that what I believe is true only in so far as it is completely false. I'm saying reality is real. You're saying it's a fantasy.

BRUTUS. Not fantasy, illusion. An illusion relies on presenting elements of reality so that the consciousness is misdirected and mistakes them for something else. This world is real, but our perception of it causes us to mistake it for something that it's not: for something permanent and final.

The other world felt more real because it was obvious that everything I perceived with my senses was fantastic, and fantasy is much more penetrable to meaning. It's like the difference between art, "a lie that reveals truth," and propaganda, which uses truth to tell a lie. Things on the other side were more true. Still, we have a purpose in being here. It's like being in a classroom. Here, we learn to be good people.

CALIGULA. Let's say that were true. Then how does it make sense that people die when they are babies? A child becomes an adult after eighteen years of being a child. But a person might die three seconds after being born, or they might live for eighty years.

BRUTUS. It's like learning to play an instrument. Some techniques are very easy, and you learn them quickly. Other techniques are difficult and take time. We come for as long as we need to make progress, and then we leave. Also sometimes I think a person comes and lives as an act of compassion. Perhaps the baby in your example is a very old soul that has agreed to live a short life to help teach a lesson to someone else.

CALIGULA. Hold on, I thought we were talking about heaven, now you are talking about reincarnation. They're different things.

JUVENAL. And they're gonna have to wait, 'cause the sound guy's here. But I would be really interested to see the little love-in between Brutus and Catullus broken up, so hows about after the show we all get polluted and see if we can convince the two of them to duke it out. Final Judgement vs. Transmigration of Souls. Ideally, to the death.

[End of Part VIII]

THIS BLOODY STAGE

A CHORUS of VULTURES.

Encore! Encore!
 Feed us more of your finest pain
Drench the air in pretty screams
 And pour us a shot of sorrow.

JUVENAL. *(addresses the microphone with a ghoulish smile)* My father always said that he wished he could have had us suckled by wolves. In honour of his wish, I give you *Mater Roma!*

(The groupies cheer. Juvenal always saves this song for last, both because it's the fan favourite and because it never fails to leave him sweat-soaked and shaken. He looks across the stage to where his former teddy-bear perches on an altar of plywood and Styrofoam. Gaius always comes to Juvenal's shows. He and Julia are the only ones who know what the song's about.

The first strains of Brutus' stand-up bass echo like thunder in the deep. Strobe lights flash across waves of bodies crushed against one another, the surging current of the Styx. From the opposite shore a woman looks at him. Her blindfolded features are utterly impassive, a sword in one hand points towards the heavens and in the other are scales piled high with bloodied coins. Juvenal struggles to focus, to remember when he's supposed to come in. There's a tangible tension. A few people in the front row have started chanting.)

CHORUS of VULTURES.

> Tell us of your Romeworld
> > The time-warp of your childhood
>
> And all that psycho-jazz
> > That's ringing in your bones
>
> Stories of love punished by suspicion
> > Tales of that sexy, sexy Roman whip

> It's never occurred to us that you were eleven
> > We never thought about the way
>
> Memory sticks to the mind
> > Like melted cling-wrap
>
> Because we don't believe a word you say

> To us it's all a pretty fantasy
> > Heavy Iron-Age torture porn
>
> Nightmare fodder for the ghastly Muse
> > Too fucked up to be real

> So come on, baby,
> > Play it hard.
>
> Make your agony sing
> > So we can dance.

(The vision of Justice begins to unwind the bandages from her eyes. Juvenal's fingers fumble the guitar strings, and feedback screeches from the monitors. Caligula beats on skins, thrashes rusted metal.)

JUVENAL. *(Screams. Long, drawn-out, with vibrato.)*

(The marble lady finishes removing the blindfold. Beneath the folds of fabric, her eyes have been gouged out. The gaping sockets stare across space, tearing it apart. The scales tip dangerously askance. Juvenal collapses.)

(It's dark.)

A CHORUS of MEMORIES.

> Remember it well, your grandfather's death-mask,
>   Frozen in plaster and fashioned in clay,
> Hung on a body of straw and obsession,
>   Placed on the shore-line to witness your shame.
>
> The whipping-post beckons, with false allegations
>   Extorts from your body its spurious wage,
> Wrenched from your silence, an unbidden wail
>   Ruffling the surface of blood-speckled water.
>
> How can you answer the ghost of a memory?
>   The scars turned to silver but never repaid?
> Can you find solace in half-wrought salvation
>   The effigy broken, the death-mask unmade?

Mother, curator of hollow-eyed hatred
　With tears on her lips as she gathers the fragments
She's hoarding the memory of shades and traditions
　While down on the boardwalk you shudder abandoned.

JUVENAL. Go away. That's all in the past. It's only a song now. *(The darkness is starting to resolve into a parking lot. There's an ambulance. The Memories retreat and the Vultures gather round, speculating on the cause of his ruin. Juvenal sits up.)* Clear these people out of here. I'm fine.

(Germanicus steps in. Juvenal is vaguely aware of negotiations taking place, ambulance attendants placing their bid on his body. Eventually he succeeds in getting hold of a waiver that delivers him from being sentenced to the hospital. He signs, a desperate scrawl. Catullus and Caligula help him to the back seat of his pick-up truck. Brutus climbs into the passenger seat. Germanicus drives.)

GERMANICUS. Where am I taking him?

CALIGULA. I can give you instructions, I know where he lives.

CATULLUS. I've seen where he lives. We're not taking him there. Maybe if we all chipped in we could afford a hotel room.

GERMANICUS. Actually, that's a really good idea. Call Julia. Tell her I'm on my way to airport to pick her up, and inform her she's putting us up for the night.

JUVENAL. Wait. Where's Gaius?

CATULLUS. It's in the back with the equipment. But I really think you should get rid of that thing, it feeds your morbid fantasies and I don't think it does you any good.

JUVENAL. I haven't slept without him since I was eight.

CATULLUS. Yes, well I don't get the impression that you're sleeping very much now.

JUVENAL. How can I sleep? There's a black hole in the moral fabric of the universe, and it's pulling at my soul. I'm pretty sure I'm past the event horizon. My only hope is that there's still life on the other side.

CALIGULA. He's delirious. It happens. If you wait, it goes away.

CATULLUS. I'm not so sure. I'll call Julia. She might know what to do.

*   *   *

(A bath. Bath is not really the right word. Font. Pool. Caldarium. The spring of eternal life. Juvenal leans back into the water and washes off the last traces of make-up from his face. The tub is palatial. Gold fittings. Soaps and lotions scented with all the perfumes of Arabia. Soft clean towels. If heaven exists, it's probably a bathtub. He pulls his head out from under the water, listens through the door to the conversation in the next room.)

GERMANICUS. I actually don't have a clear position on that. I lean towards Socrates' theory of the transmigration of souls as expounded in the Phaedo, but I think it may be flawed.

CATULLUS. My problem with reincarnation is that I don't see how my reincarnated self would, in any significant sense, be me. I have no memory of being someone else, so presumably my next incarnation would have no memory of being me. If there's no continuity of consciousness what is it, exactly, that reincarnates?

BRUTUS. Let's say you have a dream, and in the dream you're a different person, perhaps a woman, perhaps even a dragon. Your dream-self doesn't remember your waking life, and after you wake up you remember little of your dream. Yet it is still you who are dreaming.

(Waves of philosophy, as transient and comforting as the waves in the bath. Juvenal breathes it in.)

CATULLUS. Yes, that would seem to suggest that ultimately nothing that we experience in life matters very much. In a dream life is cheap. You don't feel bad, or even think twice about cutting off someone's head in a dream because you intuitively know that it's irrelevant. If life is nothing more than a very long dream what value can it have?

BRUTUS. What value does it have for a child to be in the womb? It's true that nothing you did in the womb mattered very much. You don't remember it. But without that time you could never have reached the point of being ready to be born.

CATULLUS. Yes, but when a person is born they are born into a wider kind of being. They become more individual and simultaneously less isolated. According to the Christian worldview, death continues that trend: in Heaven one is absolutely and uniquely oneself, but at the same time one participates in the communion of Saints and is incorporated into the Body of Christ. There's forward momentum towards an ultimate goal, whereas reincarnation is just a repeat loop in which the ultimate end is to escape from the monotonous refrain.

GERMANICUS. Not necessarily. Platonism is definitely directed towards a concrete final end. According to the Socratic account you want to escape from the cave in order to apprehend absolute Beauty. I don't really know Buddhism, but I think maybe the Buddha's point is that my consciousness of myself as something distinct from nature, from God, is an illusion and that this fundamental illusion is the bedrock of unhappiness.

CATULLUS. I don't care whether you give me the Buddhist, Platonist, or Hindu flavour. As soon as you start talking reincarnation you have to deny the goodness of the body, or at least reduce the body to a skin that one discards. In denying the goodness of the body, you also end up denying the goodness of matter, and quickly the world ceases to be Creation and becomes bewitchment.

GERMANICUS. Not exactly. I mean, the analogy of the cave describes the world as shadow. It's not actually bad --

CATULLUS. Yes it is. Plato's idea is that people are trapped in bodies as a punishment for primeval sin.

GERMANICUS. Yeah, but Christianity's idea is that people are trapped in fallen bodies as a punishment for primeval sin. Both acknowledge that having a normal human body basically sucks, they just have slightly different stories to explain it.

CATULLUS. No, they have fundamentally different stories. In the Christian account, our bodies are good but broken, in need of repair. In Plato's, they're bad but we have to endure them because we're broken. It makes all the difference in the world. For Plato, every time two people fall in love their embraces enslave them. Every time a mother gives birth, she is condemning a soul to prison. There's no reason to try to ameliorate human misery because pleasure appeals only to our baser nature, and suffering teaches us detachment from the world. It flies in the face of all our moral intuitions.

BRUTUS. No. Because a person must go through many, many lives before they reach nirvana, and it takes many thousands of years. Sometimes a thing that is very good along the way, like pleasure or romantic love, becomes less useful, even an encumbrance, as you draw near to the destination.

CATULLUS. But our fundamental moral intuition, the basic premise upon which all moral action is based, is the apprehension that existence is good. It's possible to imagine reaching a point, after thousands of lives, where I would be so spiritually exhausted that I would simply want to "dissolve, fade fast away, and quite forget," but I could not want that for someone that I love. To love someone is the highest possible affirmation of their being. Their individual, particular being. The lover could never will the dissolution of the beloved.

BRUTUS. But to have particular loves is a manifestation of the ego. As a person draws nearer to enlightenment their love expands so that it becomes compassion for all things as opposed to desire for particular people.

CALIGULA. No. This is bullshit. I've met these people, people who love me because they hold all of humanity in a golden embrace. They don't love me. They love the idea of themselves loving me. They love the idea of the good that they will do in my life. That's why I came to Canada, to find Juvenal again. Because he loves me. Me. Not an idea of me, but me as I actually am.

GERMANICUS. Uh...Caligula, I'm going to guess that the people you've encountered aren't actually Buddhist monks on the cusp of enlightenment. I suspect they're probably new-agers with grandiose ideas of their own spiritual advancement. Am I right?

CALIGULA. Probably. But I still think that if someone is going to love me, they have to love *me*. I don't want someone to love me because they love the cockroaches, you understand?

BRUTUS. I understand, but this is the central confusion that afflicts the person who is attached to ego-consciousness. We can't conceive of ourselves loving except as loving other egos, and we can't conceive of ourselves being loved except as egos. These are the very desires that keep us trapped in the cycle of reincarnation. We want to come back, to be individual, to relate to other individuals, but this individuality is the source of our unhappiness. That's why so often people refer to happiness or freedom as "letting go of myself."

CATULLUS. Of myself, yes. But not of someone that I love.

BRUTUS. Isn't that what grief is? Letting go?

CATULLUS. Grief. *(There's a pause. Juvenal can smell the melancholy even over the scent of tea-tree oil.)* No, I don't think grief is letting go. Accepting death, yes, but that acceptance is sustained by hope. By the thought that the separation is never permanent, that you'll be reunited one day.

BRUTUS. This is why many lifetimes are required.

CATULLUS. No! I don't care how many lifetimes I had, I couldn't accept that. That someone I love would lose a single jot of their personality, that they would cease to be a particular individual, that they would become merely a drop in an infinite ocean. It's monstrous! My entire being rebels against it.

BRUTUS. Ah. This is because love itself becomes a means of gratifying the ego through its own image mirrored in another. Yet even such a love points beyond itself. Isn't it true that lovers always wish to become one? Even in our particular loves, we long for a dissolution of the barriers that divide us.

CATULLUS. Well yes, but not in a way that simply annihilates our differences. We want to be united, but there is a massive difference between a work in which diverse threads are woven into the self-same tapestry, and an undifferentiated mass of matted wool. It is the individuality of the elements that makes it possible for them to meaningfully cohere.

BRUTUS. And it is the dissolution of the elements that finally allows them to meaninglessly coinhere. All of the highest forms of beauty are always inexpressible, their meanings flee as soon as you try to grasp them, and any attempt to impose meaning on them is an exercise in the projection of the self onto the work. It is because we wish to see ourselves in the mirror that we continue to interpret, but we come closest to the truth when we simply allow the work to be without demanding that it mean anything at all.

CATULLUS. You're mistaking mystery for meaninglessness. Mystery transcends human thought and language, but that sense which we have, that a sublime piece of music suggests a meaning which cannot be put into words, points towards a promised revelation. An unveiling. Not an unmasking.

GERMANICUS. What Brutus is trying to say is that as soon as you think you understand the meaning of existence, you've created a projection that is basically just what you would like for it to mean. In your case, your conception of the meaning of life is a macrocosm of the relationship between *erastes* and *eromenoi*, because *Eros* happens to be the idol that you serve.

CATULLUS. I deny the charges! And not because I'm transfixed by desire, but because there is one thing in the world that is worth desiring – desiring to the point of death, even dying on a cross, and that is love for another human being. "There is no greater love than this, that one would lay down his life for his friends." These are the truest words that were ever spoken, and I will not be told that the man who spoke them was egotistical or spiritually immature. He chose suffering, chose to desire the immortality of particular souls: his friends, because He saw that freedom from suffering is not the highest goal attainable to man. He aspired, on our behalf, to something infinitely greater.

JUVENAL. *(Appears at the bathroom door, dressed in a complimentary bathrobe.)* Something infinitely greater, with an infinitely greater price. And I don't just mean the crucifixion. That was peanuts. Lasted less than a day. I mean the price paid by all of the souls who are supposed to be suffering everlastingly in hell in order to make possible the beatitude of the just. 'Cause heaven implies hell. Anything else is naïve optimism. And that's my problem. I could never accept the damnation of anyone I love.

[End of Part IX]

THE INESCAPABLE NET OF RUIN

(The hotel room door opens. Julia enters with a multi-tiered tray on wheels. She's dressed in a blousy green silk thing, not really a dress, not quite a tent, that emphasizes the bulge around her stomach. Her third pregnancy. Everyone in the family has been offering sacrifice to their respective gods, hoping that this one will survive to birth.)

JULIA. Tada. *(She whisks plastic covers off of dishes, opens tantalizing boxes that release aromatic steam into the air.)* It's only carry-away, but it's the best that I could find at two in the morning. Juvenal. *(She grabs him by the shoulders and manhandles him into a brocade arm-chair.)* Feast.

JUVENAL. I take it that's a verb in the imperative?

JULIA. Oh yes. Fork. Spoon. Wait!

JUVENAL. What?

JULIA. Napkin.

JUVENAL. *(Tucks the napkin into his shirt like a good boy and tries a bite of something in a red sauce. Tastes like chicken. And coconut milk.)* We were just arguing whether heaven necessitates hell. You wanna join?

JULIA. Oh no you don't.

JUVENAL. Don't what?

JULIA. Catullus, Germanicus, Caligula – I'm sorry, I don't know your real name, just that Juvenal calls you Brutus.

BRUTUS. Li. But Brutus is acceptable.

JULIA. I want a full report on what's going on, and I want you *(she points at Juvenal)* to answer questions honestly. No more philosophical sleight of hand. But eat first. I've seen wraiths with more skin on them.

GERMANICUS. Can we talk philosophy while he eats, and then you can give him the third degree after?

JULIA. No. Because I've met you people before, and I know that once you get going on a subject you will not let it go. Also, I'll become interested and invested and I'll lose my perspective. Perspective is of the essence here. While Juvenal eats, I am going to take each of you out onto the balcony one by one, and we're going to admire the moonlight. The people inside will be responsible for making sure that this little imp doesn't eavesdrop, and that he eats his vittles. Caligula, come. I brought some Indonesian cigarettes, the ones that you like.

JUVENAL. Come on Little Boot, don't sell me out for a measly cigarette. Try to at least talk her up to thirty pieces of silver.

(Caligula shrugs as if to suggest that he is powerless, and follows Julia onto the balcony. The door shuts. It's frustratingly well sound-proofed. The green curry is delicious, but it's hard to eat with the sword of Damocles hanging over your head.)

GERMANICUS. *(his voice low)* Okay. We can have the argument now. Caligula didn't really have that much to contribute anyway.

JUVENAL. I am going to die.

GERMANICUS. Yes. But you will almost certainly not die of your older sister talking to your best friend.

JUVENAL. No. You don't understand. Julia is nuts.

CATULLUS. She's a little odd, but she's a lot more sane than you.

JUVENAL. If you say so. All right. You guys go ahead and argue. I'll try to pay attention.

CATULLUS. Well, it was your argument. You said that heaven was impossible without hell.

JUVENAL. *(Takes a deep breath, reconciles himself to the fact that he's probably better off not thinking about what's being said on the other side of the balcony door.)* Yeah, well it is.

CATULLUS. Can you elaborate that point?

JUVENAL. Universal forgiveness doesn't work. Maybe God could forgive everything but human beings don't and spending eternity with someone that you hate is not everlasting bliss. You can let in Lucretia, or you can let in Tarquin, but if you let in both then heaven becomes hell.

CATULLUS. Well yes. That's the idea behind the Final Judgement. All men may choose to forgive, and seek forgiveness, or they may choose to leave the party. It's just that there's nowhere else to go, so worms and darkness tend to prevail.

JUVENAL. So if some war criminal repents on his death bed, all the mothers who watched him murder their kids have to forgive him or they'll burn? Repenting is easy. Forgiving...

CATULLUS. That's why there's purgatory. You don't just get off free. The grieving mother is not asked to relinquish her claim on justice, she's only asked to accept that wrath doesn't have the final word.

JUVENAL. Yeah, that sounds real good in theory, but, think about what it means. Let's say that I die in a state of final penitence, and I get to the pearly gates. St. Peter brings up my record and says, "I see that in 2008 you answered an altar call and were duly dunked, so Original Sin is all paid up. Apart from that you seem to fall roughly into the Prostitutes and Tax-Collectors bracket so, good news. Front of the line." So I get in there and I track you down, 'cause apparently fags were ahead of alcoholics, and then I go looking for Caligula. Caligula's not there. He's an unrepentant murderer, and he wasn't willing to forgive the bastard that he killed. You're honestly telling me that I'm going to want to stay? Maybe I would. It's supposed to be pretty amazing, but what kind of asshole could spend eternity drinking heavenly champagne while his best friend was choking on burning coals? I would have to opt out for the sake of solidarity. I might even go so far as to say for the sake of love.

CATULLUS. Yes, I've had that thought. It terrifies me. But I think there is an answer. We talk of the saints interceding for souls, and I think what that may look like is you going down and talking to Caligula and trying to convince him, for the sake of love, to repent and to forgive. But it's his choice.

At some point you have to say, "This is what you want. I will not stop loving you but I'm not going to martyr myself to your misery forever." I think that's what's implied in the harrowing of hell. Christ goes down into the underworld, like Orpheus. He goes that far for the sake of solidarity. But He can only save the souls that are willing to follow Him out. After all, heaven is the marriage of the soul to God, and you can't force a person into marriage.

GERMANICUS. Yeah, but if the alternative is either you fall in love with God or you're tortured forever, that's definitely duress. I don't have a problem with the idea of punishment in the afterlife, but I have a huge problem with the idea that what you're being judged on is whether you said "yes" to God. Basically it means that if a person is a really virtuous atheist they suffer the same punishment as someone who was a horrible butcher, and if a person is cruel and self-indulgent but finally repentant, they enjoy the same privileges as someone who spent their entire life doing good. Even if you add in purgatory, it's still unjust.

CATULLUS. What possible meaning could there be in saying that a person is "virtuous" if they willfully reject the source of virtue?

GERMANICUS. Because your God is a person. Mine is an Ideal. For a Stoic, God is conterminous with existence, beauty, truth, nature, goodness. If you reject those things, you reject God, and if you pursue those things, you pursue God. In so far as you are judged, you are judged by the criteria of reality. Moral cause and effect. My problem with Christianity is that God has a body and a personality and He's frankly kind of arbitrary. He curses people who have willfully pursued him all their lives, and he pardons people who have blatantly broken his laws and whose only moral accomplishment is to say "Jesus! I believe."

JUVENAL. No, he curses people who have willfully pursued self-righteous pride, and he helps out folks who say "Jesus, I suck, but I'm willing to try." Even I understand that part. "He humbles the proud in their conceit, and raises the lowly." He judges based on your desire for righteousness, not on whether you had the privilege of being able to sit around in a University thinking about truth and goodness all your life. If you think that's arbitrary it's because you're totally oblivious to the relationship between virtue, especially conspicuous virtue, and privilege.

BRUTUS. Poverty and suffering do not necessarily produce evil, and wealth and privilege rarely lead people to do good. Being good is not a privilege, it's a choice.

CATULLUS. Have you two never had the experience of desperately wanting to do good, and of being completely crushed? Of being literally incapable of moral effort, in the same way that a person trapped beneath a pile of rubble is literally incapable of climbing out?

GERMANICUS. No. Because that experience doesn't exist. I've had the experience of falling down, and I've had the experience of making excuses for myself, but the only rubble that can morally crush you to the point where you literally cannot choose the good is self-pity.

JUVENAL. See? That's what I mean by privilege.

(The balcony door opens. Germanicus is summoned. Caligula returns.)

GERMANICUS. I'm not ceding the argument, I just have to go. In case that wasn't clear.

(He goes. Julia can be heard humming to herself as the balcony door slides shut.)

JUVENAL. What did you tell her?

CALIGULA. Nothing. Where you're living. What you've been doing with yourself. Some weird questions about dreams. I refused to answer about how much you drink, and I said nothing about sex.

CATULLUS. Well in that case, Juvenal is screwed. She was using the obviously invasive questions as a decoy, so that you'd feel like you were being a staunch and loyal friend and wouldn't balk at telling her the things she actually wanted to know.

JUVENAL. What are you going to tell her.

CATULLUS. The truth.

JUVENAL. Which is?

CATULLUS. You know what it is. You should also know that I've figured it out by now. I'm assuming that you've chosen not to tell anyone else?

BRUTUS. Not to tell us what?

JUVENAL. Why should I think you've figured it out?

CATULLUS. Because I was there. Also because it's obvious.

A CHORUS of MEMORIES.

> It's four in the morning, and silent Catullus
>   Is mutely descending the stair to the cellar
> Mother has told them the crypt teems with dangers
>   So Juvenal, heart-cleft, runs to protect him.
>
> He finds him there petrified, clutching his lantern
>   Wreathed in the perfume of plaster and bloodshed.

The five year old's lips are yet virgin to language,
He cannot disclose it, but still he remembers.

JUVENAL. I didn't realize you remembered... *(Juvenal draws and slowly releases a long breath.)* All right. Fine. Enough's enough. Catullus, go call Julia and Germanicus in. No, actually, I'll go get them. I could use a cigarette.

[End of Part X]

THE BLACK ASSIZE

(Afterwards, if everything went according to plan, it would be said that the room was haunted. When you were turning out the Tiffany-style lamps, and the soft click of a golden knob sounded the knell of darkness, for just a moment you would see a face beyond the window pane, shrouded by the moon. A bloody-eyed fury, scratching at the glass with a coin stolen from the mouth of the dead. For now, the lights are low. Everyone gathers in the sitting area, with the remains of a Thai feast scattered over the table. Juvenal opens a bottle of wine-dark whiskey and overfills his cup.)

JUVENAL. All right. So here's the deal. We're gonna do like Poirot, only upside down. First of all, because no murder has been committed, and secondly because the murderer-to-be is going to confess what's in his heart rather than letting our brilliant detective here *(he pats Catullus rather too hard on the back)* reveal how he worked it out. Then y'all are going to judge. A jury of the men who know me better than anyone else in the world. Jules, you get to play Athena, in case there's a tie.

CATULLUS. Interesting, but there won't be a tie. No one in this room is going to urge you on.

JUVENAL. There's the catch. You don't get to vote on whether or not I do it. Only I get to vote on that. You vote on whether or not you will acquit me when its done.

BRUTUS. I'm sorry. I feel a little lost.

JUVENAL. So listen. It'll become clear. The situation is this. About 18 years ago we found a child, freshly orphaned and wandering by the road-side, and we brought him home. He was about four, five years old, and he'd watched his father hang himself from a ceiling fan. We called him Numa because he was too traumatized to tell us his real name. So. Ostensibly, Mom got in contact with the relevant authorities and he got handed off to his aunt. We said good-bye to him, Mom drove off. Later that day, she told us not to go down to the basement because there was a dangerous leak. Later that night, Catullus and I came in to use the toilet and Catullus went downstairs. God knows why.

CATULLUS. I could hear a child crying. I wanted to know who it was.

JUVENAL. All right, so Catullus heard the ghost of Numa weeping in the darkness and followed it downstairs. There was a body there. His face was covered in plaster because a death-mask was being cast. He was dead. I'm pretty sure I remember blood. It was definitely that kid. And our mother definitely killed him.

GERMANICUS. That...I... *(It's clear that he's being rendered inarticulate by a series of emotions that are well beyond his capacity to express. He stammers for a while, and blinks a lot, and then pours himself a glass of whiskey and sits there staring catatonic into space.)*

BRUTUS. I think what your brother is trying to say is that your conclusion does not necessarily follow from the evidence that you give.

JUVENAL. There's other evidence. It's not that interesting, and she's not on trial here. Suffice it to say that I have absolutely no doubt about her guilt.

CATULLUS. No. If she didn't do it, it was Augustus, and if Augustus did it, his may have been the hand that held the knife, but hers the will that guided it. I have no doubts either.

BRUTUS. So you're trying to decide whether to turn your mother in?

CATULLUS. No. He's --

JUVENAL. Let me say it. I think it's important that I actually say it out loud, because if I can't even do that there's no way... *(He takes a deep breath.)* I'm thinking of avenging his death.

JULIA. You didn't say it. That's a euphemism.

JUVENAL. Fine. All right. I'm contemplating matricide. Is that direct enough?

BRUTUS. Why wouldn't you go to the police?

JUVENAL. A lot of reasons. There's very little evidence. I'm not a very reliable as a witness. Any half-baked shrink can diagnose me with schizophrenia in under twenty minutes. Catullus was a five year old who couldn't talk, no one's gonna believe what he remembers. The investigation would be hell for our family. Mom would probably get off, and I don't even want to think about what she would do to repay me for betrayal. Prison is a cake-walk compared to that woman's wrath.

GERMANICUS. *(Very slowly, struggling for control.)* The *investigation* would be hell for our family? The *investigation!?* That's what would be hell?

JUVENAL. Germanicus, calm down, think about it rationally.

GERMANICUS. Rationally? This is very rational. This is what we call perfectly ordinate and justifiable anger which is in accord with right reason in every conceivable way. You're talking about killing my mother.

JUVENAL. Augustus still has the death mask that they took of that kid. It's in a box in his attic, folded between old linens with lavender and bay. If this goes to the police, the only hard evidence points to him. He's got four kids and a wife. And once the authorities start prying into our family, they're gonna find plenty of leads to pursue. If the media gets hold of it, we're very picturesque. We'll be The Pagan House of Horrors. The Family from Hades. You'll still see our name on the tabloids twenty years down the road as "fresh and startling evidence" turns up.

GERMANICUS. But you think that's not going to happen if you *kill* her?

JUVENAL. No. Because like I said, any half-baked shrink will diagnose me with schizophrenia. Mentally ill people killing members of their family because of paranoid delusions is not news. It'll make the local papers. Maybe a brief mention on TV. I'll play up the crazy, and they won't dig any further. Open and shut.

GERMANICUS. But...you're missing... Shit! Why the fuck am I the only person in this room having an emotional reaction?

JULIA. Because it all was foreseen, and is accounted for.

CATULLUS. Julia, don't be portentous. I know it's in your blood, but --

GERMANICUS. Why aren't you reacting?

CATULLUS. Well I've known since the caves so I've already had my emotional reaction. I've discovered, rather chillingly, that I care a great deal about my older brother going to prison and don't give a fig about whether my mother dies.

(A beat of slowly-building tension. Glass shatters. Whiskey flows into the wounds where the fragments of an old-fashioned glass have sliced open Germanicus' tight-clenched fist. The wound bleeds, slowly at first, more profusely as he loosens his grip.)

GERMANICUS. I think I just cut myself. I'm going to go to the bathroom and clean off.

(The bathroom door closes. Germanicus puts in a noble effort, but is not entire successfully in silencing his sobs.)

JULIA. I think we'll count that as one thumbs down.

CALIGULA. Make it two.

JUVENAL. What? I was counting on you as my definite, in the bag support.

CALIGULA. Then you are stupid. What can I say?

JUVENAL. You have actually killed someone. As an act of revenge. And I shipped you half-way across the world so that you wouldn't get caught. How could you possibly judge me?

CALIGULA. It has nothing to do with judgement. I believe in realpolitik. I vote strategically. I think if I oppose you, maybe you won't do this stupid, crazy thing.

JUVENAL. Why was it okay for you, but it's stupid and crazy for me?

CALIGULA. I don't want to go into the differences, there are lots, most of them don't matter. We could split those hairs all night. There is only one that makes a difference. You can't handle it. Me. Before I kill, I worry about the police catching me. I think about how I'm going to do it. I imagine it, and I am shaking, sweating, but I smile. You? You obsess about morality. Things appear to you at night. You can't even make it through a show that you had been looking forward to for months. You are driving yourself loco, brother, and you think that this is going to stop when it is done? No. It will get worse. I vote against you, not because I care about your mother. She means nothing to me. I vote against you because I love you, and you are not the kind of man who can do this. I will not forgive you if you destroy yourself.

JUVENAL. Don't talk like you don't have a conscience. You had some pretty rough nights as I recall. But you got through them. I don't see why the fact that I want to settle the moral questions in advance means that I'm somehow different.

CALIGULA. Because you cannot settle them. You can't know what happens after death. You can't know what justice truly is. You can't know for certain any of the things that you desperately want to know. So these questions they will burrow into you like worms. I still jump every time that I hear a police siren. Why? Because I have never settled the question of whether they are coming for me. But it is a question I can live with because I can accept that one day, maybe they will come. The kind of questions that you are asking? If you are in a cell, with nothing to do but stare at the ceiling, and nothing to drink but mashed fruit fermented in your toilet? These questions will haunt you and they will be a hundred times more ruthless than your ghosts. You understand?

JUVENAL. Yeah. I think I do. I'm still not convinced I shouldn't do it, because if it's the right thing to do, if it's actually just, the fact that I am going to suffer for it is morally irrelevant. But I do appreciate your reasoning, and I accept that that's your vote.

JULIA. Catullus? Brutus?

CATULLUS. You know what I think. I agree that you are stupid, and I think you're wrong. I think it will destroy you, and I think it will tear our family apart. But I also understand. When I realized that you were talking about murdering our mother, I was surprised that I felt nothing. So I investigated my feelings and uncovered a very deep well of hatred in myself. I've put the lid back on, and I don't intend to drink from it, but I fully acknowledge that if I had sipped, even lightly, at its font it might very well have been enough to drive me mad. So if you do this terrible, idiotic thing I will forgive you. I suppose that strictly speaking, according to your rules, that means my vote is "yes."

JUVENAL. Thank you. I don't think you have any idea how much that means, and I don't think that I'm capable of being sufficiently vulnerable to express it. But thank you. *(He quickly moves on.) Et tu, Brute?*

BRUTUS. Give me a moment. Let me think. *(He folds his hands in front of him and is silent for a long time.)* You said that we were able to judge you because we are the people who know you best. I know that there's a lot more between you and your mother than you've talked about tonight. There's also the evidence of Catullus' hatred. That's a big indictment, because I've seen how much Catullus will forgive and I find it difficult to imagine what would be enough to make him hate. *(He pauses again.)* Earlier you talked about virtue and privilege. I have had the privilege of never meeting an evil person, so much so that I find it very hard to imagine that they exist. I don't know if your mother is evil. I've never really spoken with her. But I do know that I'm often unfair to you, that I find it difficult, maybe impossible to stretch my imagination into your experience and a lot of the time I act as though your decisions are just stupid and immoral without thinking very seriously about why you make them.

JUVENAL. Brutus, seriously man, give yourself more credit. You're one of very few people who will even put up with me, and I think that you quite literally saved my life. When I was at my absolute lowest point, you were the person who scraped me up off the cobblestones and found a way to get me home. And also, let's be frank and honest about it, a lot of my decisions are just stupid and immoral and my reasons for making them really do amount to...

BRUTUS. To what?

JUVENAL. I don't know. Self-pity. Self-justification. Selfishness.

BRUTUS. But I think also desperation and that's the part that I feel responsible for. It's obvious that you're suffering a lot, it's all over the lyrics of every song we play, but I don't think about it. I just think about how to turn it into good music without thinking about what it would feel like to actually live with all of that. It's a failure of imagination, and it leads to a failure of compassion. So I'm sorry.

JUVENAL. You've done a fantastic job of being compassionate. I have no complaints.

BRUTUS. I'm glad you think so. But I've known that you were in crisis for a long time, and the only thing I did about it was occasionally buy you a sandwich and try not to get irritated with you when you showed up drunk to practice. For someone whose life is as comfortable as mine, that isn't enough.

JUVENAL. Okay. If you want to blame yourself, I guess... Does that mean that you acquit me?

BRUTUS. No... To condemn you would be to condemn myself, but to acquit you would be to acquit myself. I don't have the right to do either. So it's impossible for me to cast a vote.

JULIA. That's two against, one for, one abstaining. The nays would seem to have it.

JUVENAL. Not necessarily. Gaius, what's your vote?

(Normally, when you look at the object which Juvenal considers to be his brother you get the impression that it's vaguely unsettling but conclude that after all it's only a child's craft. But once you understand its significance, you start to wonder, why is it that the paint on its crudely crafted mask ran in that particular way? Why the eyelashes, like black sunbeams on a pasty face? Why that smile, expressing anything but joy?)

CATULLUS. That's not fair. You can just make up his answer any way you like.

JUVENAL. As I mentioned last time, that's why I'm not relying on myself. Julia, what does Gaius say?

(Julia's eyes flutter. She lays her hands on the head of the strange being: half mummy, half urn, half childhood comforter, half accusing stare. Her voice when it emerges is altered, a child's piping.)

GAIUS. I say yes.

JUVENAL. Then it's a tie.

JULIA. *(snapping out of it slowly.)* I'm sorry. I didn't hear that. I think you said it was a tie? Does that mean it's up to me?

JUVENAL. Whether I'm forgiven. Not whether I do it.

JULIA. Okay. Can I make conditions? Don't answer that. I can. Talk to her. If you sit down and you ask her about what happened, and you listen to her story, the way that we've all listened to yours, and you get to the point where you understand what happened and you still think that she deserves to die, then I absolve you of whatever you choose to do. Happy with that?

JUVENAL. No.

JULIA. Good. Because I won't listen to excuses. If you can bring yourself to kill her, as an act of courage and not of cowardice, then I won't tell you that you're wrong. But if you can't even get up the manhood to sit down at a table across from her and tell her what it is that she has done, and talk to her about what you intend to do, then I will never believe that it was anything other than yellow-bellied, craven, self-indulgent fear.

* * *

(The first light of dawn stains the horizon. Inside, a pile of bodies are littered around the room. Caligula and Catullus have fallen asleep half on top of one another at opposite ends of the couch. Brutus and Julia lie splayed in the beds. Germanicus sits clutching a Styrofoam cup of cold black coffee in his bandaged hand, Juvenal's keys clutched loosely in his hand. Sleep came and overtook him in the long watches of the night. Juvenal puts out his cigarette and quietly unhooks the keys from his brother's fingers. The door closes silently behind him.)

[End of Part XI]

A BITTER DEBT OF BLOOD

(The tree under which Gaius was buried stands alone on a hill overlooking the Kirkman pastures. A white oak. The name "Gaius Majoris" is carved into the side of the tree, along with two dates, seven months apart. The date of his conception, the date of his death. Gaius Iuvenalis approaches the grave with a knife in his hand. It's the same one that his family uses to offer ritual sacrifice. The blade is freshly sharpened. He lays it down at the base of the tree where two overlapping roots embrace a circle of earth. Gaius' grave.)

JUVENAL. O spirit of my unborn brother, guardian of my life. To you I owe my body and my blood, for through your death room was made for me within my mother's womb. By your intercession, I am called to this bloody deed and I dare not refuse the debt. Therefore I consecrate its instruments to you. Obtain for me the blessings of Hermes, thrice-mighty, and bear my sacrifice in your own hands to the marble halls of Justice. Place it upon her scales, and if it lacks sufficient weight beg for me that she may overlook the difference.

(He pours a little whiskey over the soil as an offering to his brother, and then raises the bottle to his lips. He drinks deeply, surveys the knife, and drinks again.)

GAIUS. *(Seated on the ground, his back against the oak-tree)* You will return to me my stolen womb?

JUVENAL. It's not mine to return.

GAIUS. I want my mother. You've had her long enough.

JUVENAL. Is that what this is about?

GAIUS. No. It's about justice.

JUVENAL. I've done a lot of thinking about justice. Thinking about what it costs. She must be appeased, but every act of appeasement serves to whet her hunger. An impossible paradox.

GAIUS. The beggars come and kneel before her in their rags. They have lost limbs, eyes, hearts. They don't ask for anything unreasonable. Only that she restore what they have lost. From what account can she draw the debt of blood unless from that of their murderers?

JUVENAL. But if I murder our mother, won't she join the queue? She'll come in her rags, and show off her stretch-marks, and wail to Justice of how she risked her life to give me birth, and how the very hand that once stroked her breast as she nursed me came in the darkness, and in cold-blood cut her down. Do you think Justice will be deaf to such a story?

GAIUS. Why don't you ask?

(The eyes of the vision are bandaged again but Juvenal can see the trails of pus weeping from the sockets.)

JUSTICE. Do you come to pay me court?

JUVENAL. I'm here to pay a debt.

JUSTICE. *(holds up her bloodied balance)* You have many. Which do you wish to pay?

JUVENAL. I'll settle my accounts later. I've come to pay on someone else's behalf.

JUSTICE. Whose?

JUVENAL. My mother. Mary Kirkman.

(The scales dip staggeringly to the left.)

JUSTICE. You do not have enough.

JUVENAL. Cancel everything she owes me, and apply it to her other debts.

A CHORUS of MEMORIES.

He was a child then, he never committed
    Half of the crimes for which pennance was sifted.
Her expectations were piled up like boulders
    Waiting for Sysiphus' spine to support them.

At first, for a while, he strove to appease her
    But soon, as the sunburnt skin peeled from his shoulders
He threw out his spit on the ground he'd been tilling
    And cursed it for bringing forth harvests of grievance.

Lazy, she called him, ungrateful and careless

Shamelessly mocking the womb that had borne him.
The hapless usurper of Gaius' glory
  Replacing the sanctified child she had hoped for.

At night in the darkness the sheets cling like fish-hooks
  The coarse fibres twine themselves into the lash-wounds.
Tomorrow on waking he'll pull them asunder
  Tearing the scabs free from moorings of linen.

(The scales settle, still unbalanced.)

JUSTICE. It is less than the cost of a life.

JUVENAL. I know.

(He picks up the knife and drinks a little more whiskey. He looks up at the spreading branches of the tree. It's beautiful this time of year, early morning sunlight tickling the green undersides of the leaves. He permits himself a solitary tear, then grips the bottle and drinks in earnest.)

JUVENAL. Let my eyes forget what they have seen.

(He plunges the knife-point into the corner of his eye socket. At the first glance of pain, his fingers loose their grip on the knife. Bloodied water is streaming from the wound, but it's not much more than a prick. He tightens his fingers around the bone-handle once more, and this time, slowly, determinedly forces the point between the eyeball and the lid. A scream like a warrior's cry breaks from his lips as the blade slides into the cavern of his skull, prying the jellied orb from its socket. There is a dizzying moment

where he can still see through a haze of red, his field of vision split asunder, the dangling eye recording its own death. With shaking fingers, he severs the nerve.)

(Darkness. A heart-beat. The lids of his ruined eye stare open and in the hollow where his vision used to be a phantom orb gazes forth. He can see the steps of the marble palace perched on the foothills of Olympus, and Gaius standing there in a child's tunic, looking quizzically down. Juvenal's hand fumbles about in the darkness between two worlds until it finds the oozing sphere lying in the soil at his feet. He gives it to his brother.)

JUVENAL. I meant to offer both of them. But I can't do that again. This will have to be enough.

(Gaius takes the offering, cupping it in his slender hands, and bears it up the steps. Juvenal falls backwards onto the side of the hill. He opens his good eye. The tree is still there, spreading her branches into the sunlight, whispering about the glory of life as a small yellow bird flits among the leaves.)

GAIUS. (returning) Your sacrifice is not acceptable. Numa still weeps. (He profers the eyeball on a tray of brass.)

JUVENAL. Then give him my eye, and let it pour out a continual stream of tears that he may rest and be at peace.

GAIUS. It's not enough.

(Juvenal stands up, steadying himself on the tree. He can see more clearly now.)

JUVENAL. No. It's definitely enough. I refuse to be blackmailed any further by the dead.

♫   ♫   ♫

(The show isn't a big one, not big enough really to justify theatrics, but Juvenal doesn't care. The close intimacy of the venue makes him feel like he's being held, not drained by the audience but cushioned in an amniotic circle of applause. It's weird, only being able to see half the room, but the patch looks fantastic and if anyone accuses him of being a poser he can push it back and prove that he's for real.)

JUVENAL. This is the point in the show where I always sing *Mater Roma*.

(There's a burst of applause and screaming from the pit. He can see Catullus at a table, fretfully stripping the skin from the stem of a dark purple rose.)

JUVENAL. But my father is here tonight. It's the first time he's come to one of my shows so I'm going to do his favourite song.

(Jerome almost smiles, but doesn't stand up. Juvenal isn't sure whether he's enjoyed the show so far.)

JUVENAL. But first...

(Brutus draws his bow, and Caligula miraculously manages to make his rag-tag drum-kit swing. Juvenal puts down the microphone. He goes over to the altar where

Gaius perches, watching. He lays the doll down and slowly baptizes it in butane. A flick of his lighter and the flames shoot up. The paint on the face peels and blackens, and the scent of acrid smoke rises through the room.)

JUVENAL. Let the tyranny of death be ended, and the reign of life begin.

(Cue cool acid jazz. Fade.)

[End of Part XII]

www.ingramcontent.com/pod-product-compliance
Lightning Source LLC
Chambersburg PA
CBHW021356090426
42742CB00009B/886